Blessed by Autism and Other Trials of Life

A Journey in Faith and Trust

ELIZABETH NABET

ISBN 978-1-64191-836-7 (paperback)
ISBN 978-1-64258-730-2 (hardcover)
ISBN 978-1-64191-837-4 (digital)

Christian Faith Publishing, Inc.
832 Park Avenue
Meadville, PA 16335
www.christianfaithpublishing.com

Printed in the United States of America

As I look back on this journey with my son Gerard, I realized that there were three women that stood out and helped make my journey with Autism lighter.

The first two women are my Mom, and her sister, my Aunt Irene. Their love and support for Gerard, myself, and my family cannot be described in words. When things were good, they celebrated that joy with me. When times were so hard and sorrowful, they bore the sorrow with me. My thankfulness to them can only be described in how deeply I love them both. I miss them so very much as they have both passed and now reside in Paradise with God, Mother Mary, and all the angels and saints.

The third woman is my cousin Anne. From Gerard's diagnosis to the present, this wonderful woman and friend has been a constant support to me. We have received countless postcards sent to Gerard of one of his favorite places, New York City, and a multitude of books for me regarding Autism. Her sincere love and care are evident in the many phone calls asking how we were doing.

I am forever thankful to these three beautiful women who have helped me carry my cross in caring for my Gerard.

With much love and thanks,
Elizabeth

PREFACE

Blessed with Autism may seem like a peculiar title for a book that deals with one of the hardest neurological disorders to treat or understand. Parents and caretakers of these special children must learn about the many possible causes and symptoms of this disorder, but the full impact of this disease can never be fully explained in words. Even those who have chosen an occupation that relates to autism never get the full picture unless they have walked in the shoes of those who live with it on a daily basis. There are so many symptoms and manifestations that autism, along with other similar neurological disorders, has been put under one large umbrella that encompasses many different disorders. With so many different variations to this very complex disease, each child is uniquely affected.

The most important similarity in every child diagnosed is that they are all *special in God's eyes*. They may never meet the criteria of the world, but they meet the criteria of the Creator of the world. This book is about my journey with my special child. You are not going to learn about all the possible etiologies for this disease in this book. Instead you will learn about all the blessings that my family and I received, and still receive, from God for loving and accepting this special child from heaven. This book highlights many unique events from the beginning of my son's diagnosis to the present and the spiritual lessons I have learned. The greatest piece of this journey is that I have learned so much more than I could ever have imagined.

Some of the terminology that I use in this book may be foreign to a person who is not Christian. I do not mean to offend anyone. I am Catholic, and when I talk about "carrying the cross," I am referring to the cross that Jesus carried to Calvary and on which he was crucified. But this book is not just for Catholics. This book is meant for everyone from any religious background who deals with autism. My wish is to offer those affected by autism a bit of hope when life gets tough. If you receive any comfort from this book, then my mission is accomplished.

Only God knew what lay before me when he graced my son with autism. As you shall see, God was there from the beginning and helped me all along the way. I had to learn some very tough lessons before I was ready to surrender to his will. I came to understand that even on the grayest days, when you feel the most lonesome and abandoned, God is close to you. Those are days of "Footprints in the Sand": He is carrying you on those days because the weight of your cross is too heavy to bear.

The reason that I write so much about God in this book is the personal friendship I share with him. Imagine having a truly "best friend," one whom you could call at any time, both day and night. In addition, this friend is incapable of prejudice and offers unconditional love. This friendship is offered to all of us by God. Aren't we all searching for unconditional love? To be loved, even with all our dysfunctions and imperfections, is true bliss.

I am able to cope with autism because of this *spiritual support system.* The best part is that this support is available to every single soul who wishes for help. God is just a prayer away. You never have to make an appointment. There is no fee, and he never grows tired of hearing from you. Your hair may be standing up, and your teeth may not have been brushed, but it does not matter to him. Your education, your earthly possessions, your place in society does not interest him. It is what is in your *heart and soul* that God seeks to love.

Many people say, "You can't get something for nothing." I can disprove this idea: I possess no material wealth, own no fancy car, and live a rather simple life; but I am one of the wealthiest women alive. I know true happiness and contentment in a world that spends so much time and energy looking for peace and happiness in the wrong places. For example, through autism, I have discovered that my autistic son's love is *not of this world.* When he kisses and hugs me, I feel like I am actually *in* heaven. My son's trust and love for me as his mother cannot be fully described in words. He may never have a real conversation with me, yet we have communicated things to each other that words cannot express.

I will never forget those early years when autism was so difficult to handle. But if a cure were found tomorrow, I would still bless my journey with my autistic son. Because of all the difficult times we have had, God has blessed me with tremendous gifts of compassion, patience, love, and a great sense of humor. God's plan was for me to use these gifts, not just in my own home but with everyone I meet.

As you shall read, I have been blessed with many good friends in my life, but none comes close to what I share with God. It is amazing to have the "Creator of the entire Universe" on your side! With all His power, one would expect God to be very intimidating, but He is as gentle as a lamb. I have even come to see that God has a good sense of humor. He always sends me funny, lighthearted people to brighten my day when things are rough. I hope, through my stories, that you will see the joy and humor in autism too.

If someone asked me, "What is the most important lesson that you have learned since your son was diagnosed?" I would have to answer that I learned that I should not listen to the world's ideas for finding happiness and contentment. All I needed was to see life through the *eyes of faith*. Through this sight, God has revealed all the happiness and contentment that I need for the rest of my life. Although my autistic son is very dependent on me, I realize now that I needed him *more* than he ever needed me. Because of autism, I was able to step back and see what life was really about. Raising a child with autism has taught me how to live. Even with all the difficulties and troubles that we have endured as a family, I would never change the life that God has given me through autism.

PS: On November 6, 2003, my sister Ann and I traveled to Croatia to make a pilgrimage to Medjugorje, where there have been apparitions of Mother Mary since 1981. I prayed for the physical healing of not only Gerard but of all the children in the world affected by this illness or any other physical or mental condition.

CHAPTER 1

Discovering Autism

My personal journey with autism began on November 1, 1994—a day that I will never forget. It was All Saints' Day, an auspicious day, on which our third child, Gerard, was diagnosed with autism. This fact did not come as a surprise, because I already knew that. At age three, there was something terribly wrong with Gerard. At the time, I was working full-time as an emergency room nurse, but even with my medical background, I was in complete denial about Gerard's disability.

My second child, Eddie, was only twelve and a half months older than Gerard, so when I told people that I was worried that Gerard was not speaking yet, they would respond, "Little Eddie is speaking for him." The most comforting excuse I could accept at the time was the fact that Einstein did not speak until he was five, and they thought he was mentally retarded when he was in school. Although I now know these thoughts are what I call the "crazies," they gave me great comfort at a time when I hurt so badly. Ironically, I would go to work every day to help the sick become well, but I could not help my own child! My personal denial was so great that when we returned home from a vacation to Florida, three months before Gerard was diagnosed, my husband told me, "It's time to find out what is wrong with Gerard." I tried "making a deal" and promised my husband that if Gerard was not speaking by his third birthday, I would seek help. Gerard's birthday was only two days away, but I still rationalized that he had time to start speaking!

My job as a mother is very important in God's eyes, and I take it very seriously. There is not a greater gift from God than being called to motherhood, for it is the actual participation, with God, in creating a new life. Each and every day of my life, I have ended my day in a prayer of thanks, especially once my children were born. At this time, Mother Mary not only mothered Gerard, but also me! Her constant guidance and love were always apparent, but I sometimes could not feel her presence, because I was totally absorbed with my fears for Gerard and his disorder.

The pain of knowing that there is something wrong with your child is probably the worst pain in the world. The only pain that could be worse is the loss of your child. I believe that parents who have children with significant disabilities go through their own grieving process. They mourn the child that "could have been." Looking at a group of normal children playing in a playground can be a very painful experience to a parent who has not yet accepted their child's disability. Once a parent fully accepts, however, God fills the parent's heart with a different type of joy. It is a joy that some people may even find bizarre. For me, it is the feeling that we, as a family, have been *picked* by God to raise this very special child.

I remember having this feeling after the birth of my first child, our daughter Chrissy, when my husband, Ed, and I were trying to have another baby. We would go to mass every Sunday and see a husband and wife come in with their three daughters, all of whom had Down's syndrome. These three girls were so wonderful in church. I saw the love of their parents toward them, and, even more than love, I saw the dignity that they gave these three young women. It touched me every time I saw them. I thought at the time that God must have favored this couple very much to have sent them not just one, but *three* very special children. I was also deeply moved in seeing that the parents were very much in love themselves and truly happy. Seeing this family, week after week, caused me to change my prayers, and I began to ask God to send us a special child from heaven that perhaps another family could not handle or accept.

God heard my prayers and knew that Gerard would always be loved and wanted forever. But knowing, in the back of my head, that Gerard was our blessing did not help to remove the pain and fear that seemed to overwhelm me in those early days. It was easier for me to think that Gerard was just "speech delayed" and would "outgrow" whatever prevented him from acting like a normal three-year-old.

When I was planning that 1994 trip to Florida, I remember telling one of the nurses that I was having a difficult time getting Gerard to drink from a cup instead of a bottle. Unaware of Gerard's other developmental issues, my friend Kathy advised me to tell Gerard that "if he wanted to see Mickey Mouse, he would have to give up his bottle." There was nothing wrong in what she said, but it hit me like a ton of bricks. I remember going into the bathroom and crying, thinking, *If it were only that easy.* Her comment made me realize that Gerard did not have the cognitive ability to understand that treat. I did not know whether to scream or cry. All I knew was that Gerard was now turning three and I needed help.

We spent Gerard's third birthday at a block party at my sister Ellen's home. All the other kids were having a great time, but I spent the entire day running up and down the street chasing Gerard, who was oblivious to his own party. I can still see Gerard *self-stimulating*: wringing his hands and flapping them to any external stimuli with flashing lights or movement (a bicycle wheel spinning, a fan, kid's Hula-Hooping, etc.). The difficult day ended with my mom telling me we could not leave until Gerard blew out the candles on his cake. By then, my anxiety level had hit a peak; and I started to cry, and even yelled at my mom, "Are you kidding? Gerard doesn't even know it's his birthday! He has no connection to what's going on here!" When we finally left in the car, I cried the whole way home. No one can express the fear, anxiety, and despair that a parent feels at such a time.

What is so heartbreaking to many parents of autistic children is that the children often appear perfectly normal at the beginning. All four of my children have been born by C-section. My obstetrician did have some difficulty delivering Gerard by C-section because I was filled with scar tissue and adhesions, which made it difficult to get through my abdominal wall. The surgery took about three hours. Gerard had some respiratory distress following his birth, but he did not need to be put on a respirator.

So I brought home a beautiful nine-pounds-and-one-ounce baby boy. He was a completely normal baby with an excellent appetite and good sleep patterns. He made eye contact and would coo when spoken to in his baby seat. Being held and loved were his favorite activities, and I am a big kisser and smoocher. I sucked my kid's faces so often that the pediatrician thought my children had dermatitis. It actually turned out to be chapped skin from all the kissing! So the early years of Gerard's life were largely uneventful. He did not suffer from infantile autism.

We have early home videos of Chrissy, Eddie, and Gerard playing together. Gerard is looking into the camera, laughing and having a ball. But there is a particular video of ours that I have a hard time watching to this day. It is of Eddie and Gerard taking one of their daily baths where I am filming it and calling their names. Gerard is about eighteen months old and responds to his name with giggles and laughter. Three months later, on the same tape, I am filming the boys again outside in their sandbox and calling their names. But this time, I only get a response from Eddie. I repeat myself, calling, "Gerard, look at Mommy," but to no avail. Over the next few months, I would see Gerard drift further and further away from us.

We had hearing tests done on Gerard after an ear-nose-and-throat specialist literally yelled at me in his office. This specialist could not understand how I, a nurse, did not "realize" that my child was stone-deaf! He made this snap diagnosis by clapping his hands behind the chair that held Gerard. Because Gerard did not respond to the clapping, this doctor assumed that Gerard must be deaf. In hindsight, if I had that doctor right now, I would make him do a lot more than clapping his hands behind Gerard's chair. I would have told him that Gerard actually has acute hearing, but the doctor was too *boring* to pay attention to!

We had Gerard tested at a specialized speech and hearing facility. My hunch was correct. They suggested a neurological workup. On November 1, I went with my mother to have Gerard tested by a pediatric neurologist. After running a number of tests, the doctor turned and asked me, "What is your child's diagnosis?" Then I knew. I answered, "He is autistic." After we left the office, I pulled the car over and literally sobbed my heart out. My mom cried just as hard with me: her tears were not just for Gerard but also for *her child*—me!

In addition to being diagnosed with autism, Gerard was also diagnosed with hyperactivity and excessive compulsion and stimulation disorder. He never seemed to run out of energy. It was almost as if God said to himself, "Autism is not hard enough. I'll bless Gerard with a few more disorders to teach his family just how lucky they are to be blessed with him." This may be hard to understand now, but you will see just how much we were truly blessed.

After Gerard's neurological testing, my husband and I had to find the right school for Gerard. This was a long and difficult process. There was one school that we both liked very much. After Gerard's testing, the principal told us that they could not accommodate Gerard. Gerard's level of autism was considered significant and needed a different type of schooling. The principal was very kind, and she gave me a list of schools that were more suitable.

Everything that I have ever done, especially when it involves my family, is done with prayer first. I had total confidence that Jesus would only place Gerard where he belonged. With much prayer, we were finally able to have Gerard admitted to a school for the trainable mentally handicapped.

In March 1995, Gerard started school. Putting him alone on a bus at such an early age was terrifying to me. I remember that day as if it were yesterday. I cried so hard as the bus pulled away because Gerard never once looked out the window at me even though I waved and blew kisses at him. Of course, as a parent, you imagine the worst possible scenarios: he is going to act out on the bus, and they will not know what he needs! There were not enough tissues in my house as I cried to the point of sobbing, knowing that I needed divine help to carry this cross. I came to learn that the help was there, but I was unwilling to surrender all my worries, fears, and anxieties to God. I thought that by letting go, I would also be losing control of the situation. What I needed to learn was that I really could not control *anything*. When I finally learned this lesson, I was so mentally and physically exhausted that I needed rest before I could enjoy my free life! It took years of trials before I finally got it. The best part is that it is available to all of us at every moment. Complete trust in God is the total answer. As my story unfolds, you will see how God tested me and how what really mattered was the way I responded.

Now I awaken each day knowing that God will send me something new to learn, love, and reflect on. My "interior scrapbook" is full of both sad and joyous memories. What is wonderful about interior scrapbooks is that we never run out of pages! The joyous memories keep me amused on days when I feel sad and alone. Often the best memories do not come from the major events in our lives, but from the small insignificant events that make up our days.

For example, the saying that laughter is the best medicine is true. I can count many times when Gerard has driven me close to crazy; but if I stop, catch my breath, and take the time *to see the joy* in a difficult situation, I find that I am able to laugh instead of cry. If you can find joy amongst sorrow, then you have found the secret to living your life in peace and contentment. It may not happen overnight, but it is worth working toward on a daily basis.

People often ask me how I can be so happy and calm while having so many responsibilities at home. I tell them what I know to be the truth: the more difficulties and pain you are given, the closer you are to God. It is how we handle our problems that determine the outcome of our lives. I try to live each day of my life as if it is my *last*. For me, this does not mean that I am always looking for the "gusto!" Instead I look for all the ways that I can serve God each day. You cannot imagine how many wonderful gifts are given back to you for this service.

CHAPTER 2

Living with Autism

I have always been surprised that I did not receive any comfort from people saying, "You are not alone," and that there were thousands of people going through the same problems with autism. For some reason, this knowledge did not help when Gerard was in the midst of a very bad tantrum or when he pinched me hard enough to bruise my arms, abdomen, and even my breasts. The *last* thing I thought about in those situations was the people who were going through the same thing!

Autism is a funny disease in the way that it affects the caretakers, especially the mothers. When Gerard was diagnosed, the social worker in the neurologist's office gave me the phone number of a family living with the disease. The medical staff felt that this family was more experienced with autism and could possibly answer any questions that we had. I don't know about you, but I would have had so many questions that the person on the other end would have hung up on me. I never called the number. Autism can be so overwhelming, and I feared what the parents might tell me to expect up the road—it might be even worse than what I already had! So, believing that I was taking care of myself, I avoided making the phone call. You reach a level of not wanting to hear someone else's story when your own story is so painful.

Years later, my pediatrician called to ask if the mother of one of his patients could call me to talk about autism. Her son was recently diagnosed, and they were having great difficulty with him at home. Of course I told my pediatrician that I would be more than happy to talk to them. They never called, nor did at least five other families that were given my phone number to call.

The stress of autism on parents is both mental and physical. On one occasion, I met two mothers of autistic boys. One mother suffered from ulcerative colitis, and the other mother suffered from severe migraine headaches. The woman with the colitis was at home with disability benefits because she was so sick from the flare-ups of the disease. Even with all her medical treatment, nothing could relieve her constant stress and anxiety. Sleep deprivation just added to her misery. The other mom who suffered from migraines could find no relief despite all the pain medications in the world. Having suffered with migraine headaches myself, I sympathized with her. From all the stress, anxiety, and crying jags, it is a wonder that my head is still on straight!

All the physical and emotional roller coasters that life throws at us are relatively straightforward compared to autism. Autism requires special skills, ones different from anything that I had ever done before. Even with seminars on behavior modification and alternate therapies, you can never be fully prepared for what lies ahead. In the early years, Gerard's tantrums were much more frequent due to his frustration at not being able to verbally communicate his needs. Other tantrums were due to his lack of cognitive ability to reason. No matter what the cause, the actual tantrums of autism can be devastating. I remember praying during many of Gerard's tantrums. People who do not actually know autism cannot even begin to imagine what some families deal with on a daily basis.

There were so many times that Gerard threw a tantrum that I soon lost track of them. Each tantrum would have its own impact on my family and me. During the tantrum, you would feel hopeless and helpless. There were times when nothing that you did helped the situation. If I could not figure out why Gerard was throwing a tantrum, he would then escalate to behavior that would literally frighten any adult. My kids felt even more helpless as they watched me try to calm Gerard. He would start to pinch and attempt to bite. When he was really frustrated, he would bang on the walls or on anything that was close to him.

Some of Gerard's worst tantrums occurred in the car. If I were driving, I would have to pull over to try to calm him. Sometimes, he would become so crazed that I feared he would kick out the windows in the back of the car. These tantrums could be the result of something as simple as passing his favorite fast-food restaurant in the morning and not stopping to get french fries for him. He could not understand that it was breakfast time, and lunch would not be available for more than two hours. Those two hours could feel more like two years when you were waiting with Gerard.

These tantrums would also happen whenever I drove past a toy store that was close to our home. If I passed the store, Gerard would say the name of the store once, and then he would start repeating it several times. When I would say no with the name of the store, Gerard would start to wring his hands and continue to say the name over and over. He might say it a hundred times, with increased agitation each time. When he repeated the name, I would feel more nervous and apprehensive with a growing fear of "how bad" the tantrum might be this time. There were times when I would have to pull over and have the rest of my family get out of the car for their own safety because Gerard would attack whoever was closest to him in the car. He was not picky about choosing who would feel his frustration. The person sitting closest to him usually became his target.

Trying to stay in control is very hard when you are filled with fear yourself. It was times like these that left me feeling despondent and alone. I would feel abandoned by God. What I did not realize then, that I now know, is that God never once abandoned me. He was training me to become a strong woman. I had always viewed myself as being very independent and strong, but this would be a different kind of strength: strength built on trust. Trust that could not be shaken no matter what difficulties lay ahead.

In order to prevent the tantrums in the car, my husband and I would drive many different routes to familiar places in my neighborhood. This way we would not pass certain places that Gerard would want to stop. It was like planning a long and complex trip each time we went out. We needed to calculate in our minds all the places that were on the route we planned to drive. Time was a big factor since we could only pass a certain fast-food restaurant after 10:30 a.m., Monday through Friday, and after 11:30 a.m. on the weekends because only then would you be able to purchase fries and soda for Gerard. Because of Gerard's love of fries and chicken nuggets, I became a regular at that fast-food restaurant. It is pretty sad when you always have the exact amount of change ready *before* they tell you at the drive-up window. Pizza is another one of Gerard's favorite foods. My husband and I think we could have retired on the amount of money we have spent on fast food for Gerard.

It is typical of autism that a child has rigid food preferences. Gerard happens to have a wide variety of food likes. As a group, however, Gerard's preferences are not the greatest choices in terms of healthy eating, but it is the best that we can provide for him. Don't you love the people who try to give you advice on the poor eating habits of your child? Like a parent of an autistic child has a really big say in this matter! I remember one mother, at one of the autism support meetings, had a problem getting her son to eat anything but raisins and goldfish crackers. My heart went out to her. Her "loving" family kept telling her how bad her son's diet was as if she did not already know this. Like Gerard, this woman's son would smell everything he ate. If it smelled peculiar, he would not even try it. This poor mother reported that her family made her feel like she was a bad mother because she did not force her son to eat other foods. I suggested that she ask her family to come and spend the weekend at her home. Then *they* could try to feed all the healthy foods to her son. I know that would be a sure cure for their comments.

Speaking for myself, I would love it if Gerard ate vegetables and fruits, but Gerard's diet was written in stone by the age of three. He rarely eats anything different from his normal menu. So instead of beating myself up, I ask God and Mother Mary to protect Gerard from any serious illness that he could incur from an insufficient diet. I trust that Gerard will always being taken care of by heaven, and God has always provided for Gerard whatever has been needed.

As if the tantrums themselves were not hard enough, other people's reactions were far worse. I remember Gerard having tantrums in public places and looking up to see the faces of people who were not kind or compassionate. At this time in my life, I would feel tremendous hurt first, followed by anger. It is so funny how people will try to get their point across. They will talk even louder so they are *sure* you hear their condescending comments. That is *just* what you need to hear when you are trying to comfort your child and your family. My favorite comments were that my son was "so spoiled," and "Can't you control that kid?" How I wished that it had been only a spoiled child acting out. Life would have been much easier, but I would have missed out on what really mattered at these times.

We cannot change people's hearts; only God can do that. Yet there is something that we can all do. We can all show compassion, patience, and understanding to those parents we see in our community who have a special child. This applies to more than just children with autism. If I see someone in a mall that has a child who is acting out, I always offer my help. I always tell them that I am a mother of an autistic child before I ask them if they need help. This seems to break the ice. It also brings a huge sense of relief to a parent who is overwhelmed with a situation.

In those dark and difficult early years, there were three certainties that I held on to: One, I loved my child so intimately that I would literally walk to the ends of the earth for him. This also included my commitment to my husband and other children. Two, I would take care of Gerard until the day that the Lord called me home. Three, the last but most important, I knew that God and Mother Mary were sending me true blessings from heaven to keep me on the right track. In times of deep despair, they were my true hope. Mother Mary taught me to be the mother I needed to be, not only for Gerard, but also for the rest of my family. It was through God's love and the difficulties of Gerard's autism that I truly learned to live.

CHAPTER 3

School Days—Sorrow and Despair

Even though I always had a strong foundation for my spiritual convictions, I also needed to learn many lessons. Life is an ongoing classroom, and I would like to share some of the times when I could only see gray skies.

Soon after Gerard was diagnosed, I felt totally overwhelmed. My life seemed to totally revolve around Gerard and autism. Like most parents, I submerged myself into the ocean of reading material that discusses autism at great length. I attended every local meeting that was related to this disease. Every day since Gerard was diagnosed, "autism" has been a part of my home and every conversation. Autism can become such a tremendous preoccupation in your life, and daily life with autism never lets you forget that it is there. Gerard's school offered support groups for parents, so I went along with my husband to the meetings. I remember how, upon leaving the support group meetings, I would sometimes feel more depressed and afraid. There were always children who were progressing at a faster rate or who were not "as autistic as" your child. I tended to sit in the back row of the group so I could absorb the whole picture. It took me some time to truly see what I needed to see.

It is hard to believe, but even mothers of autistic children do the *comparison* game. If you are not familiar with this game, just visit a crowded playground. I guarantee that you will find it lurking among those "perfect moms" with their "perfect children." It is the moms who question or comment in a way that lets you know that their child has progressed further than your child. We have all met them at one time or another. They cannot be avoided. They try to ask about your child in a "friendly" way, but the motive is always the same. "Oh, your son isn't toilet trained yet? My son got right on the toilet and went. He's never had a problem since." How could this be? Why, because he comes from the "perfect family" with the "perfect mom and dad" in the "perfect marriage" in the perfect world. My best friend Katie calls this the "Patty-Perfect world." It does not actually exist, but it is a mirage that a lot of people like to believe in: instead of seeing what is real, you only see what you want to see. The only truly *perfect family* existed a little over two thousand years ago in the town of Bethlehem. All the rest of us have some form of dysfunction. Those who think they do not have even *bigger* issues! Do any of these Patty-Perfect mothers ever think of the feelings of mothers who have children with disabilities? Isn't having a disabled child a heavy enough cross? Ignorance should not be added to that burden. It hurts when mothers compare their children to yours, so do not be fooled by the Patty-Perfect moms because they actually have lots of *imperfection* underneath that they try to cover up and hide behind.

I realize now that the mothers of autistic children who did the comparison game were only acting out of fear. Dealing with autism is painful enough, and learning that your child is not making progress as fast as another autistic child can make you very afraid and defensive.

Some of the children in my son's school came from affluent homes. The fathers and mothers had important jobs where entertaining, both in the home and outside, were part of their daily lives. On one occasion, a mother told the group about her son's behavior involving throwing magazines on the floor and then proceeding to eat or chew on them. It was hard enough to see the pain in this woman's eyes in telling the story, but her husband's response really shocked me. He would scold her and remind her to have all the magazines in order for the arrival of guests. I could see the anxiety in her face as she told this story, and it deeply touched on my own situation: at that point, Gerard was putting anything with paper in his mouth, which included toilet paper or newspapers. As a result, I stopped having the daily newspaper delivered.

Time and again, I would go from meeting to meeting, hoping to find "the solution" to my broken heart. My other children, Chrissy and Eddie, were very young then and needed me too. So I would put on my happy face and plan time in each day for their needs. Yet the disorder of autism is capable of overwhelming every part of your life. Family and friends did not realize how much work and planning it took every time we chose to leave the house. Before Gerard, it was much easier to go out with two normal children: we would decide what to do for the day and off we would go—without giving it a second thought. But with autism, depending on the severity of the disease, you constantly have to calculate what you must bring and how much help you will require. As a result, you are often limited in the types of outings you can take and how you are going to go.

For example, if Eddie had a ball game at 3:00 p.m., the first thing I had to do was make sure that Gerard went to the bathroom. Next, looking at the time, I knew that Gerard's dose of medication from 12:00 p.m. would be wearing off, and I would have to stop to buy him a Happy Meal on the way. In my traveling bag, there had to be a pair of scissors to deal with Gerard's compulsive behavior about tags and loose strings. There was also a needle and thread in case he had a rip or hole in his clothes. Gerard can become so obsessed about the hole that he will escalate into a full-blown tantrum. The tantrum would include banging the walls or banging at his own head. Pinching and attempting to bite would follow if you were not prepared with tools for sewing—holes had to be mended *promptly!* You *cannot* forget to bring the portable CD player with all Gerard's CDs! If you forgot one CD, you were a *dead man*. If you left the batteries home when the CD player read "low battery," you would wish you were never born! A clean pair of underwear, an undershirt, and socks were also a must in case Gerard spilled anything on himself. He cannot stand the sensation of wet or damp clothes on his body, except when he is in the pool or shower. He would not give a moment's thought to taking off all his clothes in public. Finally, Gerard's books had to be brought along. Basically, you had to think of every possible way to keep this child entertained, happy, and occupied until it is time to come home. By that time, you are so worn out from chasing after such a child that you are exhausted. Beyond the physical demands, however, it was the mental anguish that truly wore me down. If I had saved all my tears during those early years, I could have filled my swimming pool. My pain was a mixture of both the physical workload and the sorrow over my lost child.

When I go to a function, I can pick out the mother or parents with an autistic child from a mile away. I can tell not from the physical appearance of the child, but by the physical appearance and effect on the parents or caretakers. For anyone who reads this book, if you know anyone who has a child with autism, please try to be as sympathetic as you can to the parents or caretakers. Unless you have walked in their shoes, you will never know how really stressful, difficult, and sorrowful their world can be. I found the greatest comfort in the most difficult times from other people who were truly compassionate, loving, and supportive of me.

During Gerard's early school days, I vividly remember the arrival of the "notebook." For those who do not know, the notebook is the direct connection between the teacher and the parents, and its contents can greatly affect the quality of your life. The teacher becomes your life preserver in rough seas, and the notebook becomes your "Bible." I do not think Gerard was halfway up the driveway before I dove into his backpack and read the day's comments in the notebook. When Gerard had a good day at school, life could not be better. When Gerard had a bad day, life was very tough. It became such a part of my daily routine that I learned not to open the backpack and read the notebook on Fridays. This way I could enjoy the weekend as best I could without the added stress of knowing that Gerard had acted out in class on Friday. So I would not read Friday's notes until Sunday night. I still feel the pain recalling Gerard's various misbehaviors at school, and I could not apologize enough to his teachers, although I knew I was not responsible for it. I always felt a sense of guilt that I was not doing as much as I could do for Gerard even though I was doing everything possible to help him.

My poor mom and Aunt Irene took on the pain of autism with me. Mom called me several times a day, and then she called my aunt to give her the rundown. If it happened to be a bad day, Mom would call not only to see how Gerard was, but also to find out how I was coping. There will never be enough words written to thank these two very special women in my life. They have been my major support system. The best part is that they spend a great deal of time each day in prayer. I always knew that they both were "storming heaven" with their prayers for me and my family throughout the years. It is only now that they truly see the fruits of their prayers. They have witnessed tremendous growth in Gerard and my family.

Had I known then what I know now, life could have been so much easier and happier. But I know that in order to really appreciate the good stuff, you have to be a survivor of the difficult stuff. Although God and Mother Mary have always been my true life preservers, I still insisted on trying to swim on my own. What I am trying to say is that, in those days, I needed to be the one "in control." I was totally consumed with trying to control *everything* related to autism. Autism has a way of taking over one's life at a slow but steady pace, but I have since learned that I gave it too much power because I was not yet ready to surrender control.

I suppose I liked what I call "carrying around the baggage." We all have a set of that emotional luggage. Some people even move up to big steamer trunks! I always tease my best friend and neighbor Katie, who has a son with a learning disability, about her "baggage." She wants very much to come to a complete level of trust in God and Mother Mary, but she still feels comfortable carrying the burden on her own. It is only when the baggage becomes too heavy and uncomfortable to carry that we are willing to leave it at the curb and let someone else do the heavy lifting. This is when God comes in and offers to carry the load.

Given all the baggage I was carrying, I should have been svelte at this time with well-defined muscles! I carried enough weight for ten people! What I needed to see was that "the baggage" was actually lessons that I needed to learn. Our burdens are *not* punishments, even though at times I would cry out and ask God, "What did I do in my life to deserve this?" The problem was that I wearing my worldly glasses with their limited vision. These glasses caused me to see things only from my own tiny perspective. Looking back, I realize I chose to see things in this limited way. The sorrow of certain events was just too painful at times, so it gave me some comfort to lash out at God and feel sorry for myself. But the comfort of blaming God was so short-lived, and the pain that I originally felt was even worse because now I also had *guilt* for being mad at God! But God does not give you guilt. We make our own guilt. One of the greatest gifts God has given me is to relieve myself of all the guilt and allow myself to heal from within.

When I think back to how I was when Gerard started school and compare that to how I live now, I am truly amazed. Then anxiety and fear were constant reminders of my daily struggle, and this has made me even more uncomfortable because I was normally a very easygoing person. My husband often teases me that when we first met, I did not have a care in the world! But with autism, my fear of the unknown with Gerard caused me tremendous fear, anxiety, and depression. I was so busy looking into the distant future instead of just taking each day as it comes. Now, by staying in *today*, I am calm and peaceful.

Gerard attends a school for the trainable mentally handicapped in Wantagh, New York. I will never have enough words to express my total gratitude for all they do for Gerard and the other students. The educators there give the kids total love, respect, and dignity—something they all deserve. School has been a truly safe haven for Gerard, where he has grown in both stature and wisdom. I never get nervous about who will be Gerard's teacher next year, because I leave that decision totally in God's hands. My constant prayer is that God sends Gerard the best teacher so that Gerard can learn, have fun, and become the best that he can be. God has always answered this prayer. We have been blessed with wonderful teachers, aides, nurses, psychologists, nurses' aides, and speech therapists. It has always been a banquet of God's blessings. My daily prayer is that God and Mary bless all those who work with children and adults who are physically or mentally handicapped. I applaud those devoted caretakers for all the work that they do to help the families of these children. For me, the children, themselves, are "God's saints" and are innocent and free of all sin. Their purpose in earthly life may not be apparent to the world, but their purpose is known in heaven.

CHAPTER 4

Autism and Its Effect on My Family

Life with autism has greatly affected my other children. If Gerard was not acting out at school, he often made up for it at home. The fact that Gerard and his brother Eddie were so close in age made the situation much more difficult. When the boys were little, Gerard had not grasped the idea of sharing, and Eddie had not grasped the idea of autism. I would often see Eddie trying to interact with Gerard but getting little or no response. It took time for Eddie to understand that there was something wrong with Gerard. In time, this under-standing led to its own healing. As they grew, all the difficult kinds of interactions that had angered Eddie in the past eventually became times when Eddie could demonstrate compassion for his brother. There were times that I believe Eddie felt guilty for being well.

In order for me to help relieve Eddie and Chrissy of the guilt they sometimes felt for being "normal," I would explain that God had not intended for them to be sad about Gerard. I told them that God's gifts are given to each of us including Gerard: sometimes these gifts go unnoticed and are not explored to their fullest potential. God had blessed Gerard in a very special way and had also blessed Chrissy and Eddie so they could become the best they could be. God wanted Chrissy and Eddie to fulfill everything that he wanted for them. My prayers were always that my children would love Gerard unconditionally on their own, without the guilt of being "made" to love him. My prayers have been heard and answered by heaven. Gerard is totally and unconditionally loved in our family.

Those early years brought much pain, sorrow, and heartache. Even as I try to remember some events to share with you, I start to cry wondering how I got through that difficult time. But I guess we all do what we have to do. Before Gerard was diagnosed with autism, my life was already quite full. My shift at work as an emergency room nurse was from 7:00 p.m. to 7:00 a.m. on Friday, Saturday, and Monday nights. One day a month, I would have to work an additional day during the week. My daily routine began by getting up at 5:45 a.m. when Eddie and Gerard were babies, ages two and one, and Chrissy was ten. While Chrissy was at school, I let the boys play outside all morning. Lunchtime came after a nice warm bath for the boys and then their two-hour nap. Because Chrissy did not get bus transportation, I could not nap with the boys but would have to wait for her arrival home from school at 3:00 p.m. Homework was done while I prepared dinner and straightened up the house. Dinner was at 5:00 p.m. so that I could be in the shower by 5:45. My husband would then drive me to work, with the kids in the car, by 6:20 p.m. Now my second job would begin: the ER was always so busy, and by 3:00 a.m., I felt like I could fall asleep standing up! At 7:20 a.m., my husband would be outside with the kids in the car to pick me up. Sometimes, that fifteen-minute drive from the hospital was the only sleep I would get on Tuesday morning until I went to bed at 9:00 p.m. that evening. The weekends were not much better. I would try to sleep for four to five hours on Saturday, but I would feel so guilty that I had not spent more time with my husband and my kids.

I would be so tired from the Sundays that I worked in the ER that I often woke up with a terrible headache from the lack of sleep. I would take two aspirins and tell myself that it was worth the lack of sleep. There were numerous times that I was up for thirty-six to forty hours without sleeping! Looking back, I think God and Mother Mary were "training me" for the times when I would be up many nights with Gerard. I truly believe that there is a purpose to all we do in our life and that nothing is coincidental. God has thoughtfully planned out all the events in my life, and the ones that bring sorrow and the pain are merely tests to strengthen me. He was actively molding and designing my soul to become what he wanted it to be.

This was my schedule before Gerard was diagnosed, but I already knew that something was not right with Gerard. I remember waking up one summer day to hear my husband calling Gerard's name over and over. My heart would break when I realized that Eddie responded right away, but Gerard had to be called several times.

Being human, we all have our breaking point and those times when we feel that we cannot go on. At that time, I remember having yelling matches with God. Not being able to feel God's presence made me feel abandoned, scared, and deeply alone. I feared that those days would never end. Bedtime became the best time of my day because I did not have to deal with what was going on in my life. It was more than depression in those early years; it was a profound sense of mourning. Even though my child was alive and physically well, he suffered from a disease that took away from the normalcy of his development. I mourned for my child. Helpless that I could not make him well, I remember bursting into tears just watching him in the playroom.

There were times I actually "battled" with God over Gerard's life. In hindsight, I was responding to my own overwhelming fear. There was no book of instructions for Gerard and the multitude of behaviors I would encounter over time. Some were so shocking and painful. One I remember quite clearly occurred when Gerard was three years old. We needed more sleeping space in our home, so we finished off the upstairs. We made a bedroom for Chrissy and a large bedroom for Eddie and Gerard to share. I also put in an extra daybed in their room because it was easier to sleep with the boys in case Gerard had to get up during the night. By this time, Gerard had already mastered the door locks and was very curious about the windows. I knew that if I were to get any sleep, I would have to be in their room. I stayed in that room regularly until Gerard was nine and a half years old. Until then, I was not comfortable leaving him alone with Eddie.

Imagine this new bedroom for the boys: there is a large skylight for extra sunlight, cream-colored walls, slate blue cottage curtains decorating the windows, and a children's wall border that I affixed around the room. A powder-blue rug and familiar character comforters on the beds made the room look so boyish and comfortable.

Gerard had just started medication for his excessive compulsive stimulation disorder. The medication caused him to become very constipated. He was also taking an iron supplement to treat a mild anemia, and the iron caused his stool to be pasty and tarry in color. Two days after the carpets were installed, I left Gerard in the playroom looking at a book while I went to use the bathroom. In those days, if I were in the bathroom for four minutes, that was a *lot* of time. When I was done, Gerard was not in the playroom. I knew Gerard did not go outside because the regular locks on our doors were now replaced with key entry deadbolt locks to foil Gerard's curiosity. We had a temporary gate on the bottom of our staircase. When I approached the staircase, I noticed the gate was pushed down. My heart pounded. I could hear Gerard babbling upstairs. Going up the stairs, I could only imagine what I would find.

When I entered the room, I did not know whether to scream or cry. I knew that screaming would not solve anything and only make matters worse, so crying was the next option, and I cried for three hours. That was how long it took for me to clean up what Gerard had left behind: he had finger-painted his tarry black stool all over the comforters, walls, white dresser drawers, and curtains. He had also smeared stool with his feet all over my brand-new carpet. I am seldom angry, and it takes quite a lot to send me over the edge. My huge feelings of anger were directed toward God more than anyone else. Poor God got my wrath that day! I remember scrubbing that carpet with boiling hot water and shampoo. The shampoo seemed to help with the smell, but even after the carpet was cleaned professionally, the stains never left. They are still there to remind me of the early years. It is so strange and amazing how something that was so hard at one time in my life seems so trivial now.

Similarly, the wall border lasted only for two weeks. In trying to get Gerard to sleep, he would become compulsive about that border.

God forbid you had a small paper end sticking out. That was all it took. Gerard pulled at that little end until the border was ripped to pieces. At the time, having to be "in control," I was determined to keep putting up the new border. What I was really doing was fooling myself. The second border ripped down in about two weeks. If I had only known then that there would come a day when Gerard would stop being compulsive about certain things that consumed him when he was younger, I would not have caused myself so much pain. Once again, I was wrongly projecting that Gerard's behavior at age three would remain the same into the future. Today, Gerard is fully potty-trained and would never finger-paint with his stool now. Now he has character borders in his playroom and bedroom that he loves and leaves intact. So there is hope for every child.

What I learned from this lesson was that it was okay for me to be angry with God. Voicing my anger to him was healthy. When my anger subsided, I was then able to tell him about my hurts and disappointments. The key was to keep talking with him and not abandon him. It never solves any problem to reject God. In difficult times, we have trouble accepting that hard experiences are allowed to happen by God, who loves us more than anything. But please know this: God only wants the best of the best for us. We get to choose our own path, and he gives us free will to choose which path. Allowing us to go through the painful experiences is God's way of preparing us for a life of peace and contentment.

What I have learned from all these tough times is to truly appreciate everything that I have been given: my family, friends, and blessings that I have received along the way. I now think of life's challenges as a *spiritual boot camp*. Those of us who make it through the difficult times become strong soldiers of God. I have personally failed boot camp so many times that it is a wonder that God has allowed me to try again. But that is the beauty of God: he keeps taking us back even when we make the same mistakes over and over. It is when you are willing to allow *his will* to take over that your boot camp becomes a success.

In the early years with Gerard, crying was a daily event. I isolated myself and my children and felt more comfortable at home than in venturing out into the world. I was afraid that being out with my children would take too much of my energy, and I did not want to face the pain of failure. I did not want to have to explain my son's behavior and then also apologize for it. During this period, I experienced the deepest sadness of my life. My heart was truly broken, but I somehow I survived it, and I did not die from autism. God gave me too much vitality to live life.

Looking back, I realize that I had been seeing my life through *human eyes* where I only saw negativity and sorrow. I was not seeing with the eyes of *faith*, which sees life's challenges as positive and optimistic. For each sorrow that is sent, a greater blessing will be received. I just was not seeing clearly enough at the time to realize this. Now I know that God has great plans for me and for everyone. We are all a daily work in progress.

CHAPTER 5

An Unexpected Blessing

A good example of how sorrow can lead to blessing was when, just prior to Gerard being diagnosed, I was injured at my job. I had been assigned to the trauma room in the ER, and it was a very busy night. Early in the morning, they brought in an elderly woman who was in cardiac arrest. While she was being defibrillated, I received an electrical shock. Suddenly, I felt my heart pounding in my chest and thought I was going to pass out. My first reaction was to go over to the sink so that I could get some water. The nurse and resident were busy attending to the patient, so I did not even mention to them that I was injured. My primary thought was that I had to get home because I knew something was wrong with Gerard and I had to look after him. I quickly said goodbye to one of my friends and snuck out the ambulance bay doors.

My husband was parked outside alone. My mother had stayed over the night before so that my husband could pick me up without the children. When I got into the car, my husband made me look at him. He told me that I looked pale and asked, "Is everything all right?" By this time, I had discomfort in my chest, and my left arm was numb and painful. I told my husband what happened. He responded, "Are you crazy? You are going back inside and getting checked out!"

My thoughts were not focused on myself, even though I was nauseous and clammy by this point. All I could think about was

Gerard at home with Mom: Mom would not know Gerard's routine or what he needed since he was nonverbal. Not wanting to lie to my husband but realizing that I needed to get home, I told him that "everything is all right," and that I needed to go home.

We were about two miles from the hospital when my heart abruptly went into a very fast rhythm with a lot of irregular beats. My husband said that now I was very pale, and I knew I needed help. He did a complete U-turn on a very busy road despite it being rush hour. Feeling so sick in the car, I thought I was going to die, but I never panicked. Years of teaching patients, over and over again, about how to remain calm and to take in slow deep breaths had paid off. All I kept saying was my prayers and asking God and Mother Mary to get me to the hospital and to *please* watch over my kids at home, especially Gerard. Gerard, at this time, would frequently throw a tantrum out of frustration at our not being able to understand his needs. I was worried that my mother would have difficulty handling him.

Upon my return to the ER, my friends immediately put me on a stretcher and followed the standard procedures. My EKG showed changes that were not in my past EKGs. The nurse who had defibrillated the older female patient also had numbness and pain in her arm up to her elbow, which subsided after a few hours. The ER physician thought I had had a heart attack. His instructions to me were to wait for my blood work and cardiac enzymes. I remember looking at him and laughing: There was *no* way I could stay! I had a family to take care of! Besides, I had Gerard!

Well, wiser heads prevailed, and I stayed in the hospital for two days. Thank God, I did not suffer a heart attack, but I was having episodes of sinus ventricular tachycardia (arrhythmia). My husband and kids survived at home without me. For those two days, all I could think about was my family and how much I loved and missed them. This was my first step in seeing things in a *different light*. I always had great devotion to Mother Mary, and saying the Rosary was always a part of my life. I said many rosaries during that hospital stay in Thanksgiving for my many blessings: for not having a heart attack, for my family being cared for in my absence, and for the good care I received from my buddies in the ER.

My coworkers took such wonderful care of me and nurtured me as if I were their own relative. I have found that working the night shift may be the most difficult hours to work, but they usually have the best nurses and crews. I worked with wonderful nurses, doctors, aides, technicians, and cleaning staff. We were like a big family. Many of us were mothers who worked these hours so that we could be home with our kids in the daytime.

After several episodes of recurring tachycardia, I was placed on medication. Returning to work after two weeks, I had frequent palpitations. Things that I had done prior to being injured now caused me to have episodes of tachycardia. Palpitations became common to me throughout the day. I found that over-the-counter medications that I used to take on a regular basis were no longer tolerable. Anything with a stimulant in it would make me ill, and the lack of sleep that had become part of my daily life now gave me a sick feeling.

In addition to my work schedule, I was up with Gerard at all hours of the night. When there was a full moon, he might go to bed at 9:00 p.m. and be up again at 1:00 a.m. with energy to spare. You could not leave him alone unattended because he would get into everything. My husband could not help at night because had to leave for work in the morning. Because Gerard would not take a nap until 2:00 p.m., the next day when Chrissy would be coming home from school on her bike, this meant that I could not sleep until that night or the next night if I were due at work. In addition to work and Gerard's needs, I had two other children and a husband to care for. I was past feeling exhausted. The only one who knew just how fatigued I was, was God.

Coming home from work, I felt dead, but I never let my friends know how often I had palpitations. During that time, I was always nervous and apprehensive, and my fears were flying away with me. Under the severe mental and emotional stress, I felt alone and began to feel despair. All I kept saying to myself was, "You have to do what you have to do." Like the mothers I mentioned earlier who had migraines and ulcerative colitis, I now had chronic palpitations from the stress and my workload. I knew I could not keep up this routine of being up all night at work and then running all day after two little energy-filled boys.

The accident in the E. took place in August 1994, and by November, we had Gerard's autism diagnosis. Nothing, however, is coincidental when you allow God into your life. He plans things out that seem, to us at the time, like the wrong choice. We like to think that we control every aspect of our lives, but when things go wrong, we blame God. But God knows what our lives need and provides it.

Here is where *faith* came in for me. One very rainy day, I was upstairs in the boys' room. I did not know what I was going to do about my work, and Gerard terrified me. Looking at Gerard playing was enough to bring tears to my eyes. I called him over and over again, but receiving little or no response. Needing reassurance and affirmation about what would happen in my life, I literally cried out to God for an answer. I said that if this was the God that my parents had taught me about all my life, he would be able to send me a sign.

My memory of that day is as fresh as if it happened yesterday. I sat on the bed thinking of an actual sign that God could send me to confirm that everything would be okay. I closed my eyes, and after much thought, I asked him to send me butterflies. It was not because I was a big butterfly fan, but the thought of butterflies just came into my head. At this point, I thought I must be really losing my mind! What I did not expect was what followed.

I cannot even begin to tell you how many butterflies I have since received. On several instances, I have walked the track, and a butter-fly has actually landed on my shoulder! Many of my major decisions were made upon receiving confirmation through a butterfly. I had never told anyone about this affirmation arrangement I made with God, but it is now close to eight years, and I am still receiving but-terflies. Today, many people know about my butterfly story, and to prove their belief, my friends and family purchase merchandise with butterflies to remind me of this wonder.

When I told a priest, who is a friend of mine, about the but-terflies, his response opened my heart and mind. He told me that the butterfly was significant in biblical settings as a representation of the Resurrection. The butterfly symbolizes how a caterpillar stays in a cocoon of darkness and lifelessness, only to be transformed into a beautiful colorful creature that is full of life. God was taking me from the darkness of despair and anguish into the light that allowed me to see the beauty of Gerard's disease.

God was ending one chapter of my life to start a new chapter. This would be the chapter about my spiritual journey in trust. What I began to learn from the butterflies was that I had to surrender things that I could not control. It was not the actual butterfly that brought this understanding to me, but the butterflies became a symbol and a reminder of the gift that God gave me: He would be there to help me in everything.

One of the outcomes of receiving my butterflies was that I received work disability benefits that allowed me to stay home and be a full-time mother to Gerard, Chrissy, and Eddie. God and Mother Mary saw that it was not possible for me to work, care for my family, and provide for the needs of Gerard at the same time. I still work very hard, harder than I have ever worked in my life, and I live with daily palpitations, chest discomfort, and pain in my left arm, all of which remind me of the gift that God has given me. On days when I have not slept enough and there is a lot to do, I still experience the same arrhythmia that I felt the day I was injured.

I realize now that I wasted a lot of time and energy worrying about things that were out of my control. I had thought I trusted God, but these difficult events helped me to develop a much deeper level of trust. This new trust is the result of a sincere *friendship* with God that words can never completely describe. The greatest part of friendship with God is that it is there for everyone.

Today, people often ask me why I am seldom without a smile or a laugh. I can smile and laugh because my friendship with God has brought me great peace. Even if I am totally "isolated," I am never *alone*. For in my heart is the warmth of friendships brought to me from heaven. Some people might think this idea is "crazy," but I have a simple response for them: "If this is what it's like to be crazy, then I choose to be insane."

CHAPTER 6

Another Blessing

Out of my injury, I received another gift from God in which I learned that people may be unkind at times, but God is always there to help ease our way.

After experiencing several episodes of the arrhythmia, I went to see a specialist who treats this disorder. I was referred to a physician affiliated with an elite group in a hospital that specializes in cardiac disease and abnormalities in heart function. After my first meeting with this physician, I left with an uneasy feeling. When I told him the story of how I was injured, I could sense that he did not really believe me or did not have the time to treat something so "trivial." The more I saw him, the more uncomfortable I became in his presence. His recommendation was that I have studies done on the electrical system of my heart. They were hoping to stimulate my heart to trigger the arrhythmia and then treat the irritated area so the arrhythmia would stop. I was to be hospitalized overnight for the study.

The thought of leaving my family at that time, when leaving to go anywhere was very difficult, made me very upset. My mom had to literally put Gerard in another room so I could leave for the hospital with my husband. I cried the whole way there, but God and Mother Mary knew my pain and sent *gifts* to relieve me of my sadness and stress.

First, as I was being admitted, I looked around and saw a familiar face. The chaplain of the hospital happened to be a priest who had been previously been assigned to my parish! He recognized my husband, Ed, and me and came right over. The chaplain blessed me and anointed me, which gave me a deep sense of peace and serenity. He promised to send someone to my room to give me Communion, which I had requested because I felt I needed all the help I could receive from God.

When my papers were in order, they brought me up to my room. The hospital was a Catholic one, so there were many different statues on the grounds. As I looked out the window of my first-floor room, I realized that I was right next to the chapel! This may not mean much to some people, but for me it was like being put next to the most prestigious estate in the world because I knew that behind the doors of the chapel, nestled in the tabernacle, was the Blessed Sacrament. For those who do not know, the tabernacle holds the Consecrated Host (the actual presence of Jesus) and the Monstrance (the vessel that holds the Host). Just looking out the window, I knew that all my friends from heaven were with me.

The last gift that I received that night came after I got settled into my room. Ed was about to leave, and I was still very worried about Gerard. Before my husband left, I went over my list for him once more to make sure Ed got everything. Now, when I think about it, the instruction list was pretty pathetic. After all the instructions about Gerard's medication and routines, I wrote over and over again for Ed to kiss and hug Gerard so that Gerard would not miss me.

As Ed was leaving, a man entered the room and asked if I would like to receive Communion (this is when the Eucharist is given and should be a time of complete reverence and quiet). I was overjoyed to see the man and welcomed his visit. Before giving me Communion, the man told me that he was in the seminary and was studying to be a priest. As the deacon held up the Host, something came over me, and I asked the man his name. This was very unusual for me, since I normally would be quiet until after I had received the Eucharist and said my prayers. His answer still brings me chills to this day. The deacon stood with his back to the open window where I could see the chapel. As he raised the Host, he said, "My name is *Gerard*, and this is the Body of Christ." At those words, my worries and anxieties about this trip to the hospital ceased. Jesus and Mary had provided a *banquet of gifts* and blessings to help me on this journey! The key was to surrender to God's ways. The poor deacon probably thought I had a loose wire, because I began crying, but these tears were for joy and not for sadness. When I explained to him about my worries for my son Gerard, the deacon confirmed what I already knew: God wanted me to know that everything was being taken care of so that I could receive the care I needed without the anxiety and fear.

The next morning, I was wheeled to the room for the heart study procedure. Upon entering the room, I saw the specialist physician, and all at once, the peace and serenity that I had felt now left me. This man gave me a deep sense of unease that did not make sense to me. After my groin was prepped, a catheter was passed through and threaded to my heart. The only anesthesia I received was a local shot that they gave me in the groin. I remember my head being turned to the side with sterile drapes on top of me. There was a large crucifix on the wall. As the procedure continued, I could actually feel the catheter enter my heart chambers. They then tried to electrically stimulate the heart in order to trigger the arrhythmia. My heart rate became so rapid that words cannot describe the feeling, and all I could do was stare at the crucifix and pray. At one point, I told God that I would be arriving to see him in a few minutes.

When the test was finished, the doctor came to my head and asked if I was waking up. The question confused me, because I had entered the room awake and talking. With a strange smile on his face, he informed me that I was supposed to be sedated throughout the procedure, but he had *forgotten* to order the sedation! Having just experienced a terrifying procedure, I realized that this doctor was definitely not the right man to help me.

As I waited to be wheeled back to my room, I questioned myself, "Why does this man treat you this way?" As I left the room, there was another woman yelling on a stretcher. They placed my stretcher next to hers, and she was in a panic. I asked her if I could help her in any way, and she told me that she had had the same procedure the day before, and they were about to go and look at the area of the heart they treated. Before the doctor came out, I quickly asked her if she had received sedation. Like me, she had received nothing and felt every frightening part of the procedure. Looking at this poor panicked woman, I told her not to let them do anything to her until she received sedation. When the doctor came out of the room, I realized that this would be the last time I would see this man.

You are probably wondering what this story has to do with autism. I believe that what I saw and experienced in that hospital was a blessing from God for accepting my child's disorder. Things that I used to see with only human eyes had been transformed so that I could now *see all the blessings* that come from disappointment, struggle, and anxiety. Although this experience had left me frightened and distrusting of physicians in general, I knew from my nursing career that there were also wonderful physicians out there and that I needed to look for one. As I always say, "You have to go through the bad stuff to get to the good stuff, or you can't really appreciate the good stuff."

In fact, when God sends you the good stuff, he sends you the cream of the crop. After being released from the hospital, I knew that I had to find another cardiologist. I prayed very hard that God would send me a woman or man that he saw as trustworthy and good. When I called a group of physicians from the hospital where I had worked, I prayed that whomever the receptionist scheduled for me would be directed by God. When the receptionist asked me whom I wanted to see, I told her that it did not matter to me.

On my first visit to Dr. Z—'s office, I realized that when we totally trust and surrender to God, he provides us with the very best. Although Dr. Z—'s schedule is hectic, with not a minute to spare, you would never know it from his manner. From the first visit, Dr. Z—made direct eye contact and truly listened to all that I had to say about my injury and the care that I had received up to that point. He made me feel as if I were his only patient that day. What I saw in Dr. Z—was what God saw in him: Dr. Z—is compassionate, kind, and very patient. My initial visit with Dr. Z—showed me that despite all the garbage you have to deal with in life, God renews us by giving us treasure as well. The blessing of having Dr. Z—is definitely the good stuff. Over the next eight years, I never received anything but wonderful treatment.

Dr. Z—helped me believe in doctors again. Over the years, a friendship has grown between us where we are able to discuss our families and life events. On a recent visit with him, I told him that the greatest thing that he has ever done for me is be receptive to my religious beliefs. Dr. Z—is Jewish. Never meaning to offend him in any way, I have mentioned Mother Mary's name many times. I try to refer to Jesus as "God" so as not to make him uncomfortable, but sometimes I slip. He has always been very accepting and makes me feel comfortable about expressing the things that mean the most to me. Each and every day of my life, I pray for him and his intentions and those of his wife and children. In my heart, I know what God saw in Dr. Z—and why he was sent to me to be my physician. There are no coincidences.

A month after I began seeing Dr. Z—, Gerard was diagnosed with autism. At this very difficult time in my life, Dr. Z—was very sorry to hear the news and was very supportive as my physician. Unfortunately, my palpitations and episodes of sinus ventricular tachycardia never subsided. But, over the years, I have realized that my injury itself is a blessing from God. Through it, I was able to stay home and raise my family. It would have been impossible to work the ER schedule at night and take care of Gerard. If Gerard were sick or unable to go to school, I had to be home with him because I could not leave him with any babysitter. He could only be left with some-one who understood autism and Gerard's special needs.

My employer's insurance company granted me disability pay through which I receive a percentage of my salary for life. This is one of the biggest blessings I have ever received because it enabled me to stay home to raise the family that God gave me. God saw the big picture when my own sight was limited to seeing only the small one. Each day, I try more and more to see things in a different way: to open my mind and heart to see things the way God sees them. Viewing life through God's eyes is so much clearer, simpler, and more beautiful than one can imagine. Yet this is the hardest lesson to learn. We all get caught up with the things of this world. That is why it is important to make time to reflect on what has occurred each day and speak to God. Tell him all your sorrows, pain, suffering, and shortcomings. If it has been a good day, tell him of all the joy and happiness. By doing this every day, you will start to see that there are less gray days and more days of joy. God will change those gray and dark days into days filled with warmth, sunshine, and butterflies.

Even on the busiest days, take a few minutes to stop and think about the negative and positive things that have occurred. I mention negative first so that you will see how the positive outweighs the negative. There are days when all I see is the negative, but today I thank God for the negatives because I see them as lessons or steps in my progress to faith and trust in God.

I grew up in a home that praised God and Mother Mary for everything, and this has helped me in my adult life. In order to understand how my relationship with God and Mother Mary started, you have to know about a bit more about me.

CHAPTER 7

My Foundation in Faith

To understand where I get my fortitude and values from, you need to know a little about my family and our past. I am the youngest of five girls, and I was blessed very early with a wonderful Mom and Dad.

My parents were married at an air force base in Sioux Falls, South Dakota, during World War II. They were very much in love, but it was terribly hard on my mother because my father was serving in the air force and was away for four years overseas. My parents were first blessed with a boy, Harold, over fifty-eight years ago. Harold died at thirteen months of age. How my mother dealt with his death was a story of incredible faith to us girls growing up. Her account of this story still brings tears to my eyes and pride in the woman that I have the privilege to call my mother.

Mom had just placed Harold, a thirty-two-pound, eleven-month-old healthy baby, down for a nap. When she went to check on him, she found him listless with fever. He was later diagnosed with pneumonia. My mother, panic-stricken, brought him to the hospital even though there were no antibiotics to treat this condition. The only medicine available at that time was sulfur. My mother watched her healthy and very active baby become weaker with each passing day. They treated my brother with sulfur injections in his thighs, which caused him to develop severe cellulitis. At this time in history, parents were not allowed to stay overnight with their children in pediatrics. So my mother would travel on the subway, back and forth, for six weeks. She said that she could hear him crying for her when she was leaving, and his little cry would haunt her during the night. Yet despite this tremendous sorrow and pain, my mother's strength grew due to her unshakeable faith. She prayed like she had never prayed before for my brother's health. Mom has deep devotion for Mother Mary, and this devotion gave Mom the peace and strength to carry this cross.

Harold was in and out of a coma during those weeks, and my father was only able to be home with Harold during the last two weeks of my brother's life. One day, when my mother was visiting my brother, she felt compelled to visit the chapel in the hospital. She looked up to heaven and told God that if he needed her son more than she needed him, then he should take him. Mom then left to go home by subway and trolley car. When she arrived home, their neighbor, who owned a phone, came to tell my mother that the hospital was on the phone. My brother had died as soon as my mother had left the hospital. God saw how much my mother loved her son, so he waited until Mom was able to bear the pain of losing him. God waited until Mom was able to surrender to his will.

Mom's final prayer to God was that my brother would never be replaced. Jesus heard her cries and felt her pain, and my mother was never blessed with another son. Instead five girls would be born to my parents, but not another boy. Over the years, my mother would tell us many times that it was her faith that made her the woman she was, and I know this is true. She is the most moral and faithful woman that I know, and I am so happy that my sisters and I are cut from the same cloth. All five of us are very strong in our religious and moral convictions, and Mom would not have it any other way.

My parents' marriage was also very blessed in that they were extremely devoted to one another, and so we grew up in a very peaceful home. They never went on separate outings nor had separate friends. They loved each other intimately, and Mom did everything for Dad. Mom would always tell us that it was because of their faith that they were so in love with each other. She said that devoting yourself to God and Mother Mary can fill your heart with so much love that people are drawn to you. What they are really drawn to is God because it is God's love that they feel in you.

Our home, along with that of my aunt and grandmother, was decorated with various Christian drawings of Jesus, Mother Mary, and St. Joseph. Each bedroom had a crucifix over the bed, but Mom would always remind us that we were not worshipping the statue or the pictures. The images were there to remind us of the constant love and protection that came from believing in what the images represented. My home, and that of my sisters, is also decorated with statues, paintings, and plaques to remind us that God's love for us followed us when we left our parents' home.

As a young girl, I always had great devotion to the "Sacred Heart" which, in Catholicism, is Jesus. In our home, the Sacred Heart's picture was in each of our rooms and was a most welcome friend. We were taught about the Blessed Trinity, the three persons in the one God: God the Father, God the Son (Jesus), and God the Holy Spirit. Many people in Christianity know about Jesus and the Holy Spirit but do not really know or understand God the Father. As a child, I could only imagine God the Father from pictures that were shown to me, usually of an old man with long white hair and a beard. In some of the pictures, his face has a stern and punishing look.

To this day, I do not remember how I began to *know* God the Father. I never heard any voices or saw any visions, but I know I had a clear introduction. Whatever it was, all the fear and uncertainties I had about the God the Father suddenly changed; and I came to see God the Father as the most loving, compassionate, merciful Father I have ever known. The tremendous outpouring of his love wiped away all the fears and misconceptions I had of him. The image I have now is still that of an old man with white hair and beard, but now I see the face of a Father who *loves* his children, and we are *all* God's children. He has taught me lessons on the importance of staying on track. If I am straying off course, he lets me know! He will give me enough rope to learn the lesson, but not enough to hang myself! My favorite part of God the Father is his sense of humor. He has sent to me some of the funniest people who are lighthearted and full of joy.

My mom's sister, Irene, and my grandma reinforced what my parents taught us at home. Aunt Irene filled our childhood with stories of the saints. Her stories were so real and genuine that you felt that she was telling about personal friends of hers who had been at her home for dinner on occasion! My grandma would fill us with stories of Mother Mary. Looking back, I realize that what they really accomplished was putting God and Mother Mary and all the saints in heaven on a human and personal level for us. They created wonderful friendships for us that would sustain us in childhood and continue into adulthood. I often say that "I am never alone or lonely because I am always in the company of God and Mother Mary and all my saint friends in heaven."

CHAPTER 8

Family Reunions

As the youngest of five girls, I was given quite a lot of love and attention. Although there is a thirteen-year difference between my oldest sister and myself, I am very lucky to have a special relationship with each of my sisters. We truly love each other, and when the five of us get together, it is magical. We giggle like little girls and find many things quite funny. Our husbands know better than to try to break us apart at a family function or gathering. They laugh at us and tell us that we are all "some pieces of work." We laugh back at them and tell them that they are just jealous because we have so much fun.

Each summer, without our families, my sisters and I go on an overnight weekend reunion to the beach. Jesus and Mother Mary bless our sisterly gatherings with an atmosphere of love, compassion, understanding, and, most of all, humor. One of my sisters owns a beautiful pop-up camper. We pack coolers of great food, snacks, and good wine.

At our first sister reunion, Gerard was only six years old. At the time, I had to anticipate everything he could want or need before I left. Unable to leave him with a sitter, other than my mom or immediate family, my anxiety level was very high. In those days, I was always the last one to arrive at the campsite and the first one to leave because I was so worried about how things were with Gerard. Back then, if the autism did not kill me, the guilt could have! My sisters would yell at me and ask me what would happen if I died tomorrow and then I realized that someone else would have to figure out Gerard without me.

Even though I knew they were right, when the dreaded cell phone call came to tell me that Gerard was banging the walls and screaming for me, I would get off the phone with a sick feeling in my stomach. In truth, I did not have anyone to blame but myself. During those very difficult early years, I tended to take "complete control" over Gerard. I thought I had to because my husband was busy at the time with Eddie's sporting events. My husband did not mean to leave me alone with Gerard intentionally, but my husband had his own fears about taking care of Gerard. It was not until Gerard was ten or eleven years old that I was able to leave my home and go to these sister reunions without tons of worry and anxiety.

My biggest mistake was that *autism is too much for any one person to handle.* We all, including caregivers, need a respite from time to time. Because of my family's financial situation, we could not afford any outside help, so I took it upon myself to take care of Gerard and my family *single-handedly.* Well, I am sure you can guess the outcome. I was totally burned out. It took me years to realize that God did not want me to carry this burden all alone. He wanted my husband and family to play their roles and help me. My husband's role was to provide all the physical, emotional, and financial support I needed to take care of this child and maintain a sense of mental well-being.

By learning to accept the support of others, which is God's *divine plan*, I was able to spend two whole days with my sisters at the 2002 reunion. This time, the cell phone was used only in case of emergency. I was the first to arrive and welcome my sisters with a wonderful glass of Pinot Grigio white wine. We took our glasses and headed for a walk along the beach before the sunset. This time, I was also the *last* to leave the reunion because I had difficulty leaving *them.* So even with autism, you can, and *should,* enjoy the normal social activities of other people by learning to take time for yourself and ask for help.

The lesson I learned was that I was entitled to a breather too. God insists on it. He knows that no relaxation makes for a very unhappy camper. Once I offered all my sorrows and disappointments to God for all the times I could not go out or was called home within minutes of arriving at an affair, I began to see things in a different light. Now, at every event I go to, I attend with great enthusiasm and appreciation, and I always thank God and Mother Mary for the privilege. I feel like a little girl going on an outing that will be spectacular.

My sisterly reunions are by far some of my best memories in my internal "scrapbook." We all travel to the Atlantic Ocean shoreline for a day at the beach. The beach might be crowded with hundreds of people, and yet I feel like we have the beach to ourselves. My sisters and I become so engrossed in talking with each other that someone could be drowning right in front of us and we might not even notice! We sit and laugh for hours at stories that we have told hundreds of times. It is funny how you can still find so much humor in stories you have laughed about so many times before. We sometimes laugh so much that people stare at us!

At our last reunion, we dined at a lovely seafood restaurant at Point Lookout in Long Island, New York. The waitress could not believe how much fun we were having. She even asked if she could stop by the campsite to visit us and asked us "our secret" for so much family love. We told her the truth: God and Mother Mary blessed this union of sisters in a very special way and provided a feast for us. Not a "feast" in the way that most people imagine: the food is great, the wine is good, but it is not about that. The feast is the peace and love that we experience during our time together. It is the humor and giggling that make us feel like we are little girls again. It is a *feast of the soul.*

At the beginning of each sisterly gathering, we start it with a prayer of thanksgiving to God and Mother Mary. We also end each day with a recital of the rosary. I believe that when you include God and Mother Mary in your plans, you are preparing for a wonderful banquet. God and Mother Mary would never provide anything less for *you.*

CHAPTER 9

Thankfulness

I learned the lesson of being truly thankful for everything at a very young age.

My parents gave us this example daily by constantly thanking God and Mother Mary for everything. From the simplest to the most elaborate things, they gave praise. Moreover, their appreciation extended to everyone they encountered. Anyone who had done a kind act, gave a gift, or sent special notes were responded to by my parents with sincere appreciation. Thanking others with a grateful heart allows people to feel your warmth and love for them. Likewise, just imagine how it must feel to God to hear a humble and sincere thank you for all the things that he does for us throughout our lives. It makes him want to shower you with more wonderful gifts of love.

By changing your focus, something as simple as going to the diner for a bite to eat can be a wonderful memory in the making. My husband always teases me about this. He tells me that we can never go out without my meeting someone or talking to someone. I cannot help myself because my gift is that I really love people. God created all of us with individual gifts and talents. Some are evident while others need to be discovered and developed. Take the time to ask God what your special gift is. He will bring it to your attention in a way that you will not be able to overlook.

Becoming a Catholic was a joyful experience that began in my childhood with Sundays. Our "family week" did not begin on

Monday morning, but rather on the completion of Sunday morning mass. My parents' devotion to God and Mother Mary was evident in everything they did. They would awaken us at 6:00 a.m. to prepare for 7:00 a.m. mass. Mom always had our dresses ironed and laid out on Saturday night, and we were showered and groomed on Saturday evening in preparation for Sunday. We never ate anything prior to mass and fasted from the midnight before. We were only allowed water to drink.

In the car ride to the church, Mom would remind us to prepare ourselves for the "most wonderful gift" we were about to receive. She was referring to the *Eucharist,* which is the actual physical presence of Jesus in the consecrated Host. It is the *greatest gift* that anyone can receive.

Before we ate anything after mass, Mom would pass around a single glass of water. We would all line up to take a sip of water to cleanse our mouth and palate after receiving the Host. We were told that by doing this simple act, we released a soul from purgatory. My sisters and I were eager to take that sip of water and believed that we were truly doing a good act for God. Even now, at the age of forty-six, I still take that sip of water after mass every Sunday. Even if sipping water does not release a soul from purgatory, God knows that my intentions are good.

After mass, we would pile into the car and head to the bakery where my father would go in and buy rolls and buns for Sunday breakfast. At home, while we were changing out of our good clothes, my father would start the bacon while Mom prepared the eggs. Although this event occurred every Sunday of my childhood, I never grew tired of it. We were all together, and that was all that mattered.

After breakfast, Mom, Dad, Aunt Irene, and my grandmother provided us with an "old-fashioned Sunday" filled with quality time as a family. This is something we seem to have forgotten in today's world. We all have such hectic schedules with even our own kids: Who is in what sport? Which one needs a ride here or there? Before you know it, the weekend is gone, and you are right back at work again. Before long, our children grow up, and we do not realize where all the precious time has gone!

My parents always prepared a big meal for Sunday dinner when we were growing up. It was always served between 2:00 p.m. to 3:00 p.m. at our home or at my grandmother's house. Mom or grandmother would roast a fresh ham, roast beef, or leg of lamb each week. My sisters and I would spend lazy Sunday afternoons as a family, and we would not leave our grandmother or aunt's home until we had all watched the Ed Sullivan Show and the Wonderful World of Disney. Oh, how I loved that tradition! To this day, I still make a roast, turkey, or a special meal on Sunday. I love to cook and bake, and we all eat on good china in the dining room. The preparation of a nice meal brings me comfort and allows me to continue my childhood tradition with my children.

My grandmother and Aunt Irene's homes were filled with so much love. Aunt Irene never married, so we were like her five daughters. She would let me play with all her costume jewelry and dress up every Sunday. She never yelled at us or even complained that we had made a mess in her room. They were so glad to see us each week. These Sunday gatherings were also a confirmation of their love and devotion to God and Mother Mary as they gave each of us love and the sincerest warmth. These are my treasured memories. I often think that God knew what lay ahead of me, so he built a strong foundation in me as a child. It became a foundation so strong that it could withstand all the turbulence of my adult life.

I have tried to keep some of the traditions of the past with my own family: one is that we eat as a family every night at our kitchen table. I do not allow the kids to take a plate into the family room or their bedrooms. If they want to eat, it has to be with the family. We come together each night and talk about each person's day. It is a time for good conversation and for touching base with the important issues that have come up in the day.

Another sacred tradition is Sunday dinner. I usually serve dinner around 2:00 p.m. to 3:00 p.m., and, unless the children have made other plans, my kids are present for a real family dinner. It is *our time* to spend with each other, outside of our hectic schedules. The best dinners have been when Chrissy and Eddie have given me a list of what they need to make dinner. Then they take over my kitchen and work together to prepare a wonderful meal. I know this tradition has had a powerful impact on my children because when they talk about happy memories, they are usually centered on eating around the family table. After dinner, they all disperse, but they leave with a sense of peace and fulfillment. We all need some old-fashioned tradition in our lives. It is a vital key to peace and contentment, and the renewal of family life and tradition.

Another blessing from my parents was the family rosary. Some people make fun of the rosary, and that upsets me. But, instead of feeling angry, I feel very sorry for these people because they do not understand the importance of this simple prayer and how it brings many strong graces and blessings. By "reciting the rosary," you are marking the journey of Jesus's life from the time of his conception to his death on the cross and his resurrection. People today yearn to find true contentment: why does one person, who has many difficulties, have a smile and finds joy in living while another, with similar difficulties, becomes despondent and depressed? I believe that to find true joy and peace, you need to know God. Those who seek joy and peace from other sources know only the material world. For me, reciting the Rosary brings me closer to God and Mother Mary. It brings comfort when you feel your world crumbling, and there is no light at the end of the tunnel. Many people think that the Rosary is just for Catholics, but it is for everyone. Later in this book, you will see how this beautiful prayer changed a life that was so very close to me.

By the time I was four, I learned how to say the Rosary. Each evening, we sat as a family to pray the Rosary. Mom would lead us while my father tried to catch the eye of one of his five girls to make us laugh when it was our turn to say the decade. This was a very comical moment and very typical of my father. My father was a fun, lighthearted man, who was blessed with remarkable talents of his own. His personality drew a crowd wherever he went. People could not get enough of my father, and now I realize that it was his sense of peace and joy that drew people to him. He died of a massive coronary at the age of fifty-two when I was fourteen. I took it very hard. Like everyone else, I was drawn to my father's joy and serenity.

Some of you reading this book may not be able to relate to a happy childhood or have never felt close to God. First, I would like to express my deepest sympathy for you. To all those who have shamed, humiliated, oppressed, and abused you, shame on them. I know that such familial abuse is a vicious cycle that repeats itself over and over again if no intervention is taken. Although I may not completely understand your pain, God and Mother Mary know. They are your *true parents* in heaven and love you more than you could ever imagine. There is no wound so large that cannot be healed by a loving God. Mother Mary is our mother in heaven, but she is also *here* on earth to fulfill the void that some biological mothers leave. It is never too late to seek them in your life and start the healing process. All you need to do is ask, and, in time, you will begin to see your life in a different way. Remember we are all children of the Creator of the universe, and we each have our own personal journey to take. God and Mary are always there to smooth out the rough spots and fill our journey with love, joy, and, most importantly, peace.

CHAPTER 10

Heavenly Friends

As a Catholic, I have many "friends in heaven" who are more commonly known as the saints. In order for you to understand my personal relationship with these heavenly friends, you need to know what they have done to earn the title of friend.

Let me begin with St. Joseph. I cannot tell you how many times my toilet was blocked by toys being flushed down by Gerard. You might say to yourself, "Why didn't you just lock the bathroom door?" If only life with autism were that simple! Trying to keep the bathroom door shut in our house is nearly impossible because, with six people, the bathroom is in constant use. Making sure the bathroom door was always closed became a full-time occupation in our home. We even went so far as to put a Christmas bell on the doorknob so that I could hear when the door opened. This became a problem when guests, like Chrissy and Eddie's friends, came over. I would hear the bell, run over, and start banging on the door, yelling at Gerard to open the door when it was *not* Gerard inside! No matter how many times I explained to other people the meaning of the bell, they still looked at me like I had ten heads on my shoulders! Eventually, the bell came off, and we went back to having problems with the toilet.

Autistic children love to watch things go around and around. Well, imagine that you are autistic, and you can see your favorite toy characters going around and around in water. That was what Gerard saw when he flushed his toys down the toilet. This was probably the ultimate in enjoyable stimulation for Gerard. I can imagine him wringing his hands with joy as he watched his toys go to their watery grave.

By now I had spent a lot of money on professional plumbers who came to my house to snake the line clear. It is pretty pathetic when the plumber knows you by your first name. The great fun for the plumber was asking me what character was in the trap. He found it all quite amusing, but I did not find it funny when I had to pay two hundred dollars each time! It was two hundred dollars that I did not have. I decided then that I needed some divine intervention.

My husband went out and bought a mechanical snake for our toilet. Although he tried for some time to clear the blockage, he was not successful and eventually gave up. I then took the snake, and, starting with a prayer to St. Joseph for help in getting the toy, I tried to open the drain. My husband began laughing at me and shook his head like I was a little crazy to be praying for a blocked toilet. He stopped shaking his head when I pulled the toy out of the drain! We still laugh about it at home because it is amazing how many times a prayer to St. Joseph has worked. Now if the toilet gets clogged from a large amount of toilet paper, my husband hands me the snake and tells me to ask St. Joseph to help out. St. Joseph is the saint that I call on when anything needs to be repaired in our home. He was a master carpenter and has helped me in my home many times. My love and respect for this saint has led me to name my youngest son Joseph. Who knows, my son may one day grow up to be a plumber!

Another saint, St. Anne, helped me with a different problem regarding Gerard. Toilet training Gerard took over six months. Every fifteen minutes, my egg timer would go off to remind me that I had to take Gerard to the bathroom. The two of us spent more time in the bathroom toilet training than most people spend in their entire lives! Gerard's school had asked me not to put rubber pants over Gerard's underwear while training him: I always followed the directions from the school to the letter. The hardest part of training Gerard was that it happened during the winter, which meant that I had to change all his clothes several times a day—every time he had an accident. I constantly prayed to God to give me the patience and endurance I needed to not only complete this task, but to fulfill my role as a mother to this special child. Those six months felt more like six years to me.

One afternoon, I went to the church to pay a visit to the Blessed Sacrament in the tabernacle. I began "talking with God" and remember being quite assertive and asking, "Why isn't Gerard catching on to toilet training?" I am not crazy, but I could almost swear that I heard a soothing voice tell me to "pray to the Mother and Grandmother." This strange comment actually made perfect sense to me. I realized that the things that mothers usually concern themselves with on earth, "Mother" Mary took care of in heaven. Likewise, Mary's mother, St. Anne, is also the "grandmother" of Jesus. In front of the Blessed Sacrament, I promised that I would ask for Mary and St. Anne's help in my prayers. Within three days, Gerard urinated in our bathroom by himself! Since then, Gerard has never had even a small accident! We all need Mother Mary and St. Anne to intercede at Jesus's throne. Their prayers come with the special love of a mother and grandmother: after all, how could their Son and Grandson refuse what they ask of him?

Another heavenly friend that I have is my pal St. Anthony. He is the patron saint for finding lost things (and getting you that parking space right in front of the store in a very crowded mall!). Most Catholics know about the extraordinary power of this special saint, but to me, St. Anthony is much more: he has been a lifesaver on many occasions. Caretakers of children with autism understand the emotional upheaval that occurs when an autistic child has misplaced a toy to which he is abnormally attached. There are no words that can console or explain to an autistic child that the toy is lost. If the toy is not found within a very short period of time, you will literally wish that you could disappear or die before the tantrums start. Deep down, you know that these are *not* options, so you proceed to look under every piece of furniture in your home. The search cannot be limited to the child's room or playroom, but extends to every part of the house.

Talk about family togetherness! My whole family ends up on their hands and knees looking for the toy. An added "reward" is that while you are looking for the missing toy, you might receive complimentary pinches from Gerard. At this moment, his voice becomes extremely high-pitched, wavering between a cry and a full-blown scream. His tantrums could go on for well over an hour if you are unsuccessful in finding the missing toy. You can try to do all kinds of behavior modification, but Gerard will escalate past the point of no return. Eventually, Gerard would fall asleep after throwing a tantrum for hours. It was during these severe tantrums that I became the most fearful and sorrowful.

In these circumstances, I needed divine intervention. So I began calling St. Anthony's name loud enough so that he could hear me from heaven. My call was sometimes in a voice of despair because the toy emergency might happen at 7:00 p.m. on a Sunday when the local toy store had already closed—so there was no hope of sending out my husband to get a replacement copy of the lost toy. In these cases, my plea to St. Anthony was for him to search heaven, find the toy manufacturer, and send an identical toy to me. Sometimes, before I called St. Anthony again, the toy that I prayed for would just show up. The toy would often be found in an area that we had already searched! This found toy always seemed to be a bit *newer* than the one we lost. Having witnessed this so many times, I know that these are *small miracles*, gifts from God, sent with much love. Just as you might thank a friend for a kindness, I thank all my saint friends repeatedly for these wonderful gifts of love and compassion they send to me and my son Gerard.

CHAPTER 11

Special Saints

One of my *special* friends in heaven is St. Philomena. You probably have never heard of her before, but she has become a very special part of my life. One afternoon, I received a large postcard in the mail. It had a painted portrait that I thought was of a Native American girl. I was struck by her beauty, and I turned to the back of the postcard to read about this saint. She was not Native American, but she had died as a teenager and as a virgin martyr for God. Very moved by the physical beauty of this teenage girl, I proceeded to put this postcard in Eddie and Gerard's bedroom. There was a small prayer on the back of the card for her intercession. For people unfamiliar with the word *intercession*, it means that this person goes before God on your behalf to ask that your intentions and prayers be heard and answered if it is in God's will.

Each day, while making the beds, I would glance at the picture and ask Philomena to pray for Gerard's healing. One of the things that struck me about the postcard was that Mother Mary had told other visionaries that "nothing is refused to little Philomena." At the time, Gerard was having a very difficult time at school. He was very agitated with frequent outbursts of bad behavior. My pediatrician saw Gerard a lot more than he probably wanted to! Those office visits, in the early years, required tranquilizers—not for Gerard but for me! I dreaded taking Gerard to the doctor's office because Gerard's normal behavior would transform into violent acting out because of his overwhelming fear. Gerard was completely out of control in those days.

My pediatrician could find nothing wrong with Gerard and ordered a CAT scan of Gerard's head under sedation to rule out any growths or abnormalities. This put me under severe stress! From the time the test was ordered to the date it was taken, I aged ten years. My fears flew out of control, not over the possible results, but over how I would get Gerard to the hospital and have the scan done: Gerard had already been home from school for two weeks because all he did was pinch, attempt to bite, and punch everyone. He was very agitated. His stay at home was not recommended by the school but a decision I made. How could I send Gerard to school knowing that he was going to behave very badly? Keeping him home protected the other children and staff from Gerard's outbursts.

My sister Ellen came to help me take Gerard in for the test. At the time, my husband was also in the hospital recovering from a second knee replacement surgery. I think my husband was a bit relieved to have missed this "opportunity" of taking Gerard to the hospital. Ellen remained calm and collected as she watched her younger sister, me, start to unravel at the hospital! We could not stay in the hospital waiting room because Gerard was getting progressively more agitated and fearful. He wanted no part of this place. The medical staff did not call for Gerard for over two hours. The only thing that seemed to calm him a little was telling him that I would take him to the store to buy toys afterward.

Gerard's hands were, and still are, very dry and even calloused from his frequent hand wringing. Looking back now, I can laugh at my sister's attempt to calm Gerard by massaging his hands with cream. There she was in the middle of a hallway in a large hospital, creaming and massaging Gerard's hands. He was annoyed with her but realized it was a no-win situation. My sister is as headstrong as Gerard. It was pretty funny, and Ellen and I laughed in the midst of my fear.

After "massage therapy" was over, I decided to take Gerard to the bathroom before the test. Still laughing about the touch of Gerard's softer hands, we walked toward a couple holding a baby in the hallway. The baby was about ten months old. Knowing that Gerard loves babies, I walked to the side of the couple and the baby. Gerard passed and quietly said, "Baby," and his hand reached out gently to lightly pat the baby on her head. His hand never reached her head. It was intercepted by the mother's hand. In a nasty, angry voice, she told me to take my son's hand away from her baby. Both parents looked at Gerard with disgust.

There was not enough toilet paper in the bathroom to dry all my tears! When I left the bathroom, the couple was gone and had probably been called in for their baby to be scanned. My face and eyes were red enough to let my sister know that something had happened, but I could not even get the words out without crying. I wanted to leave right then because it was all more than I could handle. Ellen looked at me and said, "Let's pray for those parents. Their baby is being scanned for some medical reason. Maybe they can't handle it, so you took the brunt of their fear."

Even though I knew she was right, my hurt and anger made me want to lash out at them. After taking a breath, we joined hands and prayed three prayers: Our Father, Hail Mary, and Glory Be. By asking God to heal me of this anger and hurt, I started to feel the pain of those parents. As he has done so many times before, God turned a painful situation into a blessing. We also prayed that Gerard would be somewhat cooperative when it was his time to be scanned.

Two minutes later, the door opened, and out came the nurse to explain the procedure. She was an angel from heaven: she was warm and compassionate to all of us. What happened next, however, still amazes me: we had just finished praying that Jesus and Mary would help Gerard be cooperative and calm, but were surprised when Gerard seemed to go into a *trance*. Gerard went into the room as if he were being led. He sat down on the X-ray table and raised his sleeve over his elbow. The nurse applied a tourniquet, started an IV, and administered the sedation, causing Gerard to fall asleep right away. My sister looked at me with an expression that no words can describe and just said, "Wow." Later, I remember leaving that room in a state of confusion. There is no other way to describe what had happened: it was a *miracle*. Gerard was *not* the same frightened child that I brought to the hospital hours before.

When his scan was over, Gerard walked over to me and said, "Momma, I go bye-bye Mommy's car, get toys." He was very groggy, but he remembered what I had promised him.

Because the scan took place during the weekend, the results would not be available for twenty-four hours. So I was all alone for another stressful weekend of Gerard being very agitated. He would bang his forehead with the palm of his hand as if to tell me that his head was killing him. Gerard's behavior was so out of control that I could not visit my husband, Ed, in the hospital for more than an hour a day.

In the early morning, I would go to help bathe Ed and wash his hair. It was all I could do for him at this point, and Ed knew that there was something terribly wrong with Gerard. Ed did not expect any more than I could give at that time, and my mom came to stay with me while Ed was in the hospital.

On Monday morning, I was on the phone at 9:00 a.m. sharp with my pediatrician. The CAT scan was normal. Thank God, no growths or abnormalities were noted. Gerard's sinuses were open with no impaction. But despite the good news, I became more upset. Gerard was still not behaving like himself, and his behavior did not improve. Mom sat at the kitchen table, watching me cry out of complete frustration. Where was I to go now?

I do not know what brought me upstairs to Gerard and Eddie's room. When I entered the room, I was startled. The picture of Philomena, which had been on their dresser for months, was now standing upright against their window in the middle of the window opening. Earlier that morning, I had locked their bedroom door after bringing the boys down for the day. It surprised me so much that I wondered how the picture got there. Being so upset, I decided to pray to Philomena for help. I finished my small prayer and proceeded downstairs. Forgetting all about the picture, I went about my normal routine. But it was a difficult day because I was still very anxious not knowing what was wrong with Gerard.

That afternoon, Eddie came home from school and ran upstairs to change from school clothes into play clothes. He was not upstairs more than thirty seconds when I heard him yell for me as he flew down the stairs. He was pale and looked like he had seen a ghost. Eddie kept repeating that the picture in the window was looking at him and he saw her face change into a smile. I then asked him if he had put Philomena's picture on the window. His said no and had thought *I* put her there. I went upstairs, took the picture, and put it on the kitchen table where I examined her carefully. I saw no physical change, but I felt that God was sending her to help me with Gerard.

The next morning, Gerard was still very agitated. Looking at Philomena, I asked, "What am I to do?" I did not hear any reply, but I felt this strong need to call the hospital to discuss Gerard's CAT scan with the radiologist. I wondered about my desire to do this. After all, I trusted my pediatrician completely. The more I looked at St. Philomena's picture, however, the more I wanted to make that call. Even my mother questioned why I needed to call the radiologist. All I know is that when God wants something done, move out of his way! He will move mountains to help you.

Nervously, I called the hospital and was connected to their X-ray department. A middle-aged woman answered the phone. I explained to her that I had received the CAT scan results and asked if it would be possible for the radiologist to review them again. Then I told her the entire story about Gerard's change in behavior. Hearing the stress in my voice, she pulled the films for review.

A couple of minutes later, she told me that the radiologist reviewed the scans again but saw no abnormality. The woman continued to speak to me in a very sympathetic voice and then paused and asked me if Gerard had lost his top front baby teeth. I told her no. Gerard was eight at the time, and they were still in. She told me that the CAT scan showed an upper baby tooth that was impacted in the gum and the second tooth was trying to come out. She could see that his tooth was being blocked. Before I could say another word, she explained to me that she had just started in radiology about a week ago. Before that, she was employed at the hospital's dental clinic for autistic children!

The woman then made me get off the phone and touch the area she described to see if it gave Gerard discomfort. I did as I was instructed, and, bingo, Gerard almost bit me because of his pain. She advised that the tooth be pulled out, or it could result into an abscess and create real problems. There were not enough words to thank her.

When I got off the phone, I thanked God for sending me St. Philomena, whom, I know, led me to that call. Philomena's work was not over. The last time Gerard had gone to the dentist, it involved *three and a half hours* of general anesthesia to have all his baby molars capped so they would not develop dental rot and toothaches. Gerard might need a specialized dentist for the impacted tooth and he would not be eager to open his mouth.

Looking once again at Philomena's picture, I asked for her intercession in heaven. My prayer was for her to loosen Gerard's tooth so that I could extract it. Gerard had experienced two and a half weeks of uncontrolled behavior and sleep deprivation and was not happy about it. I tried wiggling the tooth, but it was imbedded in the gum with no signs of loosening. Now my faith had to come, and I needed to trust beyond trust. Both Mom and I stormed heaven with prayers for St. Philomena's help.

The next morning, I woke up to Gerard standing over my bed, pointing to his tooth and repeating, "Mama, tooth." Immediately, I jumped out of bed to remove the tooth that would not even budge the day before; it was now wiggling in his gum! Did this surprise me? Not really. Faith is the most important trait that I possess, and this experience confirmed, once again, that everything is possible with God.

This baby tooth was embedded, and it looked like the gum was growing over the tooth. Gerard allowed me to wiggle his tooth enough so that it could be pulled out by the time we had lunch. The minute the tooth was gone, Gerard returned to his old self. His agitation left, and he returned to school.

As for St. Philomena, I realized how powerful this little saint is in heaven. She has been such a good friend to me that my daughter, Chrissy, had her art teacher do a charcoal sketch of Philomena. This was given to me as a Christmas present and hangs in my hallway so that I am constantly reminded of Philomena's miraculous powers in my own home.

All these heavenly friends are available for you too! Do not be afraid to explore the greatest friendships you will ever know. The best part of these friendships is that they are eternal, and there are no strings attached. My saint friends are so kind to me that I can carry on a full conversation without ever hearing a verbal reply. Talking to them brings me a sense of tranquility in times of despair and need.

As an added bonus, that Sunday at mass, I prayed for God to forgive me for the anger that I felt toward the couple in the hospital. My next prayer was for their baby and that all was well with her. While at mass, Gerard kept turning around in the pew. After repeatedly doing this, I turned to see what he was looking at. Behind us was a young couple with a beautiful baby girl. I immediately thought of the angry couple in the hospital and hoped that God would not put me through that again. Gerard kept saying, "Baby," and I kept telling him not to turn around. But there were just not enough toys to distract Gerard from wanting to see the baby. I even prayed that God would speed up the mass so that we could leave soon.

At the end of mass, the mother of the baby came to our aisle. Her beautiful smile complimented her beautiful soul as she introduced her baby to Gerard. I did not know what to think! I told her what happened at the hospital, and then she asked Gerard to sit down, which he did right away, and she proceeded to place her beautiful baby girl in Gerard's lap while still holding her for support. Gerard was in heaven: his face radiated with absolute joy. Of course, he smelled the beautiful strawberry blond curls, which added to the baby's beauty.

What a lesson for me to learn! God had shown me that there were good people to help me carry my cross: the receptionist in radiology and this young couple to name a few. It was a renewal of my faith in mankind. When one couple caused pain, God sent me another to fill my heart with joy. I was so thankful for God's outpouring of love that I thanked this couple many times. Afterward, when I ran into this mother in the grocery store, we would always remember that important day. These joyful moments are *banquets* from God.

One never knows when to expect them, but they are given as a wonderful surprise from our very loving Father in heaven.

Last, but not least, is the saint for whom Gerard is named. My mother was introduced to St. Gerard over sixty years ago by my aunt Dot's obstetrician. Aunt Dot had developed toxemia at the very end of her pregnancy. Her blood pressure became so high that she convulsed prior to delivery. My mother witnessed my aunt's severe convulsions that caused bleeding down her cheek from biting her tongue. It was so dangerous that the doctor came out to the waiting room to ask my uncle Jim and mom to pray for my aunt and the baby. The doctor told them to pray to St. Gerard because he is the patron saint of mothers. Mom and Uncle Jim stormed heaven with their prayers for the intercession of St. Gerard. We all believe that Aunt Dot and her son James came out well, thanks to good St. Gerard. This testament to a saint's intercession made St. Gerard a lifelong friend to Mom. As a result, Mom has sent countless novenas and medals to women in pregnancy, or those having difficulty getting pregnant, or difficulty in keeping the pregnancy.

St. Gerard is so well loved in our family that two of my nephews have the middle name Gerard. Each time a daughter became pregnant, my mother would start pleading that we name a son "Gerard." After my third C-section, I called Mom on the phone in the recovery room and told her that she finally got her "Gerard." She was thrilled. She did not know that I intended to name him Gerard from the beginning.

I also have great devotion to St. Gerard. Many times, I have given out medals or novenas to women having difficulty getting pregnant, and, within a short time, they often become pregnant. I always tell them to spread the devotion by giving the medal or novena to someone else who is in need of St. Gerard's help. It does not matter what religion you observe: the saints are for everyone.

For example, once when I was still working at the hospital, I was assigned to the gynecological floor. I had a Jewish patient named Sarah, who was very depressed after losing her third child to miscarriage. The doctors had ruled out any gynecological cause, and they could not figure out what was wrong. There were no words to console this very heartbroken woman. I told her a little about St. Gerard, even though I knew that she probably was not interested. I was wrong! She was so deeply sad that she was very receptive to any hope. She was discharged later that day, and I took down her address. When I got home from work, I placed a medal and prayer card, along with a note of consolation and reassurance that nothing is impossible to God. I included my name and address and reaffirmed that I would pray for her and her husband.

Time went on, and I continued to pray for her, but since I did not hear from her, I assumed she did not get pregnant. I was wrong again! Exactly one year later, I received a beautiful birth announcement with a picture of a delicious new baby boy. Sarah and Phil had a healthy baby boy that they had named Gerard! I was a little shocked that they had named their firstborn son Gerard, but I was not surprised that St. Gerard was doing his job once again. Sarah's beautiful letter was filled with so much joy that I could see her face smiling while reading it. Her pregnancy had been uneventful, and she had a wonderful labor and delivery. Most significantly, she gave complete credit to St. Gerard for helping her. Sarah and her husband had said the prayer on the back of the prayer card each night together. Their way of thanking St. Gerard for their miracle baby was to name him after this very powerful saint. The baby's name would be a constant reminder to them of the power of heaven. Sarah, Phil, and baby Gerard moved to Florida shortly after my own Gerard's birth. Although I have lost contact with them, I know I am always connected to them through our mutual friend, St. Gerard.

CHAPTER 12

Lessons for My Other Children

It surprised me that I never missed returning to work in the ER. Although I missed the wonderful people who worked there, I knew we would always be friends. To this day, if I go to the hospital, the ER staff always makes me feel loved and welcome. This was a great blessing because God knew I needed good friendships and wonderful memories to sustain me in my new "employment" at home. The work related to autism, along with the stress, was enough to keep anyone from missing the ER. After a hard day of dealing with Gerard, I would fall asleep at night in less than a minute. My husband teased me that I fell asleep *before* my head hit the pillow.

Within a year of Gerard's autism diagnosis, he grew rapidly in both size and strength. During the next few years, Gerard would have his worst tantrums and behavior. He was increasingly frustrated that he could not communicate his needs, and his behavior became more and more aggressive. Soon his tantrums were an everyday occurrence. During these outbursts, Gerard would reach up and grab a piece of skin from any person nearest him. Then he would pinch and twist the skin. He particularly liked pinching me under my arms. I had multiple bruises, not only to my both arms but also to my breasts. People used to stare at me in the summer months because my arms were so bruised. If my husband and I were at a store, people would actually give my husband dirty looks, thinking he was the cause of my injuries. I chose to take the brunt of Gerard's pinching and biting because I had to protect my other two children.

But no matter how much I tried, there were times when the moment my back was turned, things happened so quickly. Although Chrissy and Eddie got their share of pinches and occasional bites, they were always protective of Gerard. They have tremendous love for him and have always treated him with complete love and respect. Both Chrissy and Eddie voluntarily took the name "Gerard" as their Confirmation name at age twelve. I tried to talk them out of using that name because I feared they chose it out of guilt. But they assured me it was not guilt but their unconditional love that helped them make that choice.

In return, Gerard gave us his own unconditional love. I often tell people that Gerard is *not of this world*. I mean this in a positive way: all the things that we human beings get caught up in have no effect on Gerard. His connection to the world is through total trust and love of his family and the others who care for him. He asks for very little: a certain food, a book, a video game, or a tape. His sense of time comes from attending school and seeing the changes in the way our home is decorated for the holidays. Looking back, I realize that Gerard did not need us as a family: we needed *him* to save us from going through life with the limited vision of the world instead of the wonderful insight we have through faith.

My other children have witnessed more dreadfulness than many adults with respect to Gerard's outbursts of behavior. I used to fear that this would have a negative effect on their lives, but instead my children have benefited from having Gerard as their brother. It is difficult for many people to understand that when your autistic child is behaving well and lovingly, the feeling you have as a parent cannot be matched. It actually helps heal your pain from the bad outbursts and gives you the strength to carry on.

Because of Gerard's autism, there is a true bond between my children. Although Chrissy is eight years older than Eddie, the two of them have a wonderful friendship that I know will support them throughout their lives. Both have deep compassion for Gerard and try to include him in their plans whenever they can. Often, they will plan activities together at home. For example, on Fridays, they usually rent a movie and just hang out together as sister and brother. They never fight or argue, which I think is an effect of having Gerard in their lives: Chrissy and Eddie do not want to waste their time or energy, because they appreciate every moment of peace that they are given. In their love for Gerard, Chrissy and Eddie always bring something home for Gerard to make his day more fun and pleasurable. Chrissy and Eddie also extend their love and understanding to their youngest brother, Joseph. Joseph, my fourth and youngest child, is too young to fully understand Gerard and autism. Joseph knows that something is "not quite right" about Gerard, but Joseph accepts Gerard's behavior as "normal." As Joseph has gotten older, Chrissy likes to take him out in the car to places that he enjoys.

Because Gerard likes to play video games, Eddie has had to play some of them over and over with him—to the point that one worries that Eddie might become angry with Gerard. Instead, I often hear Eddie's beautiful soft voice, reassuring Gerard that everything is okay. There have been many times that I have had to call Eddie home from a friend's house to help Gerard finish a level on a video game. You might think that Eddie would come home with a long and angry face, but Eddie always greets me with a smile at the door, saying, "It's okay, Mom. We weren't doing anything special." I have gone so far as to question my friend Katie, who is the mom of Eddie's best friend, whether Eddie gets upset when I have to call him home for a few minutes. Katie tells me that Eddie always says that it is okay and leaves immediately. I have tried to learn some of these video games to avoid having to call Eddie, but no matter how much I try to master them, I never have any luck.

I remember going to support groups about autism and hearing parents say that their other children had trouble handling the sibling with the disability. These parents would complain that their children fought all the time. This gave me food for thought. The reason my children do not fight is simple: from the time we learned about Gerard's condition, I prepared my children on all the different aspects of autism. Most of this information would frighten an adult, let alone a child! But I added this most *important* lesson: whatever Gerard does or however he behaves, *God is there* to help us in the situation. From the start, I taught my children that Gerard is a *true blessing* in our home and he is our ticket to heaven. God gave us Gerard as a *gift*, and it is our duty to show God what we are able to do with this gift. There are no truer words that I have ever spoken to my children, and they have taken this gift very seriously. They have all become Gerard's advocates. They laugh with him, correct inappropriate behavior, and even tell him to knock it off when he is out of control. They always come to him in the truest sense of love, dedication, and devotion. As a result, my children are the "jewels" in my crown: they have carried the cross of autism and now see all the joy and happiness that Jesus and Mary have sent us through Gerard.

In return for all their love and devotion, God blesses and sends graces to each of my other children. Chrissy, Eddie, and Joseph all possess their own gifts, talents, and strengths. They know all the problems and difficulties that we have endured as a family, and this has made the foundation of our family that much stronger. My children often tell me that they have learned tremendous lessons from Gerard. The most important lesson, I feel, is that they have learned is to be able to sacrifice with love. This is a very hard and difficult lesson for even an adult to learn! It is with deep satisfaction that I can honestly say that my children have mastered this. There were many times, especially in the early years, that we could not go to certain places because of Gerard. If we tried to go, there were lots of things that had to be done or procedures that we had to follow. This is very difficult for any child to accept, but God and Mother Mary allowed my children to see Gerard in the way that heaven sees him. My children are able to see Gerard as a blessing, and not just as a sacrifice and disability. This precious gift will always be theirs and help them become compassionate, patient, loving, and caring adults.

With this sacrifice of love, God also blessed us with the *gift of patience*. Autism requires a great deal of patience: patience for Gerard and patience for the rest of my family. But God's patience cannot be bought or demanded; it only comes to those who sincerely ask for it. By asking God to share in your life, he will replace your anxiousness and fear with a sense of calm and peace that cannot be described. But people around you will start to notice because they will feel God's peace and hope in you. People often ask me how I can be so patient and calm. The answer is simple: I am not walking this journey alone. My dearest Friend is right by my side, holding my hand and encouraging me to stay on track. I am never afraid of what lies ahead, because he has already planned the way for me.

CHAPTER 13

Defending Gerard

Chrissy and Eddie are Gerard's best protectors. Even though Gerard does not understand when someone is making fun of him or acting in a cruel way, our family absorbs the pain of it. There have been several instances where Chrissy defended Gerard against some of the cruelty of the world. I should begin by telling you a little about Chrissy. Our daughter, Christine, is a very bright, enthusiastic, and beautiful young woman. She always tells you exactly how she feels, even if you do not want to hear it! "Popular" should have been her middle name: she draws a crowd wherever she goes. Although Chrissy's behavior was difficult to deal with during her teenage years, she has always had sincere compassion and love for her brother Gerard and the rest of her family. As she emerges into adulthood, it is easy to forgive the freshness and arrogance that characterized her teenage years. In those days, her outspokenness often got her into trouble even when she spoke the truth! In other words, Chrissy will not put up with nonsense from anybody.

Gerard was about four and a half years old when this story took place. We live across the street from one of the town pools. There is a lovely park that adjoins the pool area, and it was a great help to me, when my kids were young, to be able to go across the street and enjoy the park with its slides and swings. Gerard would stay on the baby swing for hours while I pushed him back and forth. Because the pool was very crowded in the summer during the morning and afternoon hours, I would wait until my husband came home to take the boys across to the pool in the evening. I was unable to manage all the children alone at the pool, because Eddie was only twelve months older than Gerard, and Gerard was still at an age when he might run off on his own.

One day, my husband called from work saying that he had to work overtime. Chrissy, who was about thirteen at the time, was home, so I asked her and her friend Marilyn to come and help me take the boys to the pool. Dinnertime was the best time to go since most people were at home eating. Gerard was very excited about going to the pool, and he flapped his hands so much that we could almost have "flown" over with him! He was always so happy to have this special outing each evening.

The park had a large baby pool that was separate from the main pool. As soon as we got through the park gates, Gerard jumped right into the baby pool. Gerard's ability to make eye contact is minimal, so he soon was in his own little world at the pool. The sheer joy on Gerard's face was more than any mother could ask for. He would smack the water with his hands, causing the water to splash on himself. He would laugh and laugh about this in complete enjoyment. In general, it takes very little to make Gerard happy, and the simple things in life bring him the most joy. Despite his autism, Gerard truly *understands* the secret to enjoying life.

On this evening, I left Chrissy and Marilyn to watch Gerard and Eddie in the baby pool while I quickly went to use the ladies' room. There was only one other little girl with her mother at the baby pool. I was in the bathroom for less than two minutes and was just walking out when I heard Chrissy's voice yelling at someone. The lifeguard was sitting calmly in front of the boys, so I knew that the lifeguard was not getting balled out. Then I saw the woman who was with her daughter in the baby pool. When I reached the pool, Chrissy was letting the mother have it with both guns!

Believe me when I say that Chrissy does not hold anything back! When she is angry and wants to tell you something, she will find your weakest point and drive the message home. Apparently, when Gerard was splashing himself in the water, the little girl was also getting wet. Although this was a large baby pool that can accommodate many children, the mother came over to Gerard and told him to stop splashing. Of course, Gerard paid no attention to her. Chrissy then told the woman that her brother was autistic and that he did not understand. I guess this explanation was not good enough for this woman, because she then proceeded to go over to Gerard and splash him in the face with water that she had cupped in her hand. That was her big mistake: Thank God Chrissy was only thirteen and a half years old at the time!

The first one I looked at when I reached the pool was Gerard. There he was sitting in the baby pool without a care in the world. He radiated such joy and happiness, and had no idea about what had just happened. Chrissy, who still remembers this woman distinctly, lashed out and told the woman over and over again about Gerard's autism. When I tried to intervene on the woman's behalf, it was useless. Being only a teenager herself, Chrissy made this woman look like a reprimanded two-year-old! As I mentioned earlier, Chrissy can be brutally honest, but she is also very funny at times, so I tried hard not to laugh when I really should have been chastising her. Her comments to this woman were focused in a way that was intended to hurt the woman in the same way that Chrissy felt hurt. Tears followed after Chrissy's anger subsided—tears of hurt that anyone could be that cruel. I explained to Chrissy that not everyone is going to be kind and understanding of Gerard or his disorder.

It later occurred to me that I had always taught my children to find God in each person they met. How was Chrissy to find God in this woman? If I could not find God in this woman, how could I expect my children to? I brought the matter to a prayer. That Sunday at mass, the priest of our parish delivered his homily. It was about finding God in our neighbor or the people whom we come in contact with in our daily lives. I almost fell off the pew! This was just what I had asked God in prayer, and this sermon has stuck with me ever since. The priest said that it is really impossible to find God in those who are cruel, abusive, nasty, offensive, and downright rotten. You are not going to find him there, and you are not supposed to; what you are supposed to see is what *God* sees in these people. God sees the *whole* picture. He sees the pain, suffering, anxiousness, fear, and dysfunction of the person that have caused them to become unpleasant. This was real food for thought. It made me look at people in a completely different light because now I knew that I did not have to spend my time looking for something that I would never find. When I started to look for what God sees in them, I started to see their pain.

This episode reminded me that there is no prayer that is not heard and answered in heaven. The way it is answered may not be to our taste, but it is what is best for us because it is God's will. My husband and I could not be more proud of Chrissy when she later had to make a very important life decision. As I said before, God hears every prayer. He just answers them in ways that we never expect, and often his surprise endings are the best. What saddens me most is that some people do not wait for the surprise. They give up—at the beginning, the middle, or near the end. Their anger or disappointment in God is caused by the fact that they do not see his help coming immediately, or perhaps their prayer was answered in a way that was different from what they expected. It was not until I learned to completely surrender that I was totally filled with the joy of living in God's will.

My son Eddie is the opposite of Chrissy. Eddie is very quiet and reserved. When Eddie speaks, I listen because he has great wisdom for his age. From the time he was a small boy, Eddie helped and served his brother, Gerard, and the entire family. Although he rarely asks for anything for himself, Eddie loves to eat, so when he wants something special, he usually requests a favorite meal. He receives everything with the sincerest gratitude: it may be something as simple as making a nice breakfast or having his friends over for a meal and then watching a movie. He never goes to bed without giving me a huge kiss and hug and a very sincere thank you.

Besides being a wonderful, loving, and compassionate son, Eddie is an outstanding brother. His love for his family is fierce, and he spends a great deal of time with each of us. As an honor roll student at school, Eddie has written several wonderful essays about our family. Gerard loves Eddie in a very special way: although they are unable to have a real "conversation," Eddie always knows what Gerard wants or needs. If we are out in public, Eddie is never embarrassed to take Gerard's hand and walk him into or out of the bathroom. Both Eddie and Chrissy see Gerard through the eyes of faith and know how blessed they are to have a special needs child as their sibling.

Eddie is a young man who has sacrificed a lot out of love for his brother, and he is a truly humble servant of God. Eddie's own faith is rock solid, allowing him to keep *me* on track when the days seem long and overwhelming. He always gives me a big kiss and tells me to keep my faith, saying, "God has never let us down, and he never will." Out of the mouths of babes comes profound truth and wisdom!

God never fails to reward the faithful. Eddie has been blessed with many gifts and talents. Besides his academic achievements, he is also a very good athlete and has won several awards in baseball, football, and soccer. But you might never know this from speaking with him, because he is very humble.

Our fourth and youngest child is Joseph, who has enough curiosity for ten children! Joseph was also speech and developmentally delayed, and when we first recognized it, I thought my husband was going to have a stroke! Now we had to cope with another child who had a serious problem! I tried to reassure my husband by reminding him that this problem does not change Joseph's sweet nature. At the time, my husband could not understand how I remained calm and still found humor and laughter in the situation. The reason I had hope was always the same: I cannot change God's will, but I have the choice to accept it with obedience and love, or fight it with anger, sorrow, and depression. I decided to do what is needed with a "joyful heart," rather than go through difficulties with an angry and confused one.

Our neurologist diagnosed Joseph with persuasive developmental disorder, and this diagnosis enabled us to get Joseph all the proper therapy he needed. He goes to a school in our district for developmentally delayed children and receives speech and occupational therapy. His teacher and two teacher's aides have worked so well with him that now he cannot *stop* talking! They tell me his is like a "sponge" because he absorbs everything that is taught to him. As a family, we prayed the Rosary every night for Joseph's steady progress in school. As always, God knew what we needed, and Joseph has had a wonderful year in school. He will remain in the program for another year and then be reevaluated.

The way I see it, God thought we did such a good job with Gerard's significant autism that he decided to give us another child with a much milder version so that we would be sympathetic to families of children with less severe autism. Each day, I can see Joseph's cognitive abilities increase, allowing him to communicate his needs and follow directions better and better. Joseph is the most lovable five-year-old, and he loves to be hugged and kissed—and around me, all my kids get smooched constantly. I have always made it a part of my daily routine to spend special time with each of my kids. It is vital to their social and mental health. This way, if I have to spend more time with Gerard at a given moment, I do not feel guilty, and my children do not feel neglected.

By contrast, my husband, Ed, sometimes has had a hard time accepting Gerard's disorder. This may be because Ed also has had a more difficult time learning to completely trust God. Although Ed has very strong religious convictions, he tends to be the kind of person who needs to *see* in order to *believe*. I am *not* judging him in any way; he is a very faithful and loyal spouse, and his love for his family is boundless and is the center of his life. But there are times he wishes he could be as calm about the disabilities as the rest of us are. I did not fully appreciate what Ed was feeling until I prayed for God to reveal it to me: Ed's greatest fear is *what will happen to Gerard* after we die. This fear is very real and palpable. Most parents of autistic children have the exact same concern. I personally try not to dwell on this reality—not because I am in denial but because of my complete trust in God. I have little financial wealth to leave for Gerard, but I am at peace knowing that Gerard will always be looked after by God.

Most readers may think that I must be "crazy" to have such trust, but it is not crazy when you open your eyes to the wonders that God unfolds before your eyes. God and Mother Mary have *never* let me down—*not once* in my life. From a very young age, I learned that God answers every prayer in his own good time and according to his own will. He has already given me so much, and I know that he will continue to do so throughout my life. Each day brings a learning experience from God, which, in turn, brings me wonderful gifts. This process is true for everyone when you let yourself see it.

Whenever Ed becomes anxious and worried, I ask him if his constant worrying changes or solves so much as *one* thing. He usually responds, "I can't stop myself from worrying about tomorrow." I then tell him, "How can you worry about tomorrow since God has not created it yet? I never look back, because it is in the past and I cannot change it. I live for today, and stay in the day that I am in. Each day has its own set of troubles to deal with, and it takes too much energy to worry about tomorrow, which may never come. I only look for what God wants me to do today." Living with autism and a full household is certainly enough for anyone to think about for one day!

It makes me sad when Ed gets nervous and upset when we discuss Gerard. Ed has not reached that level of peace that my children and I have. He often wishes he could be like us, but it is in his nature to worry. He openly admits that God has always taken care of everything we needed, but he still clings to the belief that you have to take care of some things on your own. In my daily prayers, I always pray for the "lukewarm" souls, souls that have *drifted* away from God and do not believe they need God in their lives. It makes me sad to contemplate the loneliness of such people. But it is never too late to invite God into your life. Once you allow God in, you will receive profound help for your child and yourself. I know that God will eventually show my husband how not to be nervous and afraid. God will teach Ed how to let go of dysfunctional fear and anxiety, and fill him with a beautiful sense of trust and peace. God *wants* to help us with every aspect of our lives; we just have to invite him in!

CHAPTER 14

Unexpected Gifts

After Chrissy's confrontation with the angry woman at the pool, Ed and I decided it was time to try to put a pool in our own backyard. The town pool had been a wonderful treat for us until I gave birth to Joseph. Now with four kids, it became impossible to pack them up, escort them over, and watch them all simultaneously at the town pool. By having a pool in our own yard, Gerard could enjoy the water whenever he wanted, and the rest of the family could enjoy time together in the summer.

Our backyard is a good size, but it had a deep downward slope. I warned the woman at the pool installation company that my backyard was so slanted that my kids could go sleigh riding in our backyard! When the pool installer came to inspect the yard, he laughed and told me that it would take weeks by shovel to flatten the yard, and a backhoe was needed to dig out the area for the pool. After calling contractor after contractor, I found no one willing to do the job, so I brought this matter to serious prayer. I went into my bedroom and faced the crucifix on the wall: "You blessed me with Gerard. Now I need someone to dig out the yard! Please tell me whom I should call."

Heading back to the kitchen, I had one contractor's number left to call. A young man answered the phone, and I explained our circumstances. I was so desperate this time to find someone that I mentioned Gerard's autism, which led to a discussion about children in general. The young man told me that his name was Mike, and that he and his wife had recently been blessed with a healthy baby boy who was now five months old. Mike explained that he and his brother owned a large contracting firm that cleared large pieces of land for malls, grocery stores, and minimall complexes. His equipment was too large to be used in residential neighborhoods. We continued to talk, and I told him that I had brought this matter to prayer, and his firm was the last number that I had. I could hear in his voice that he was sorry about not being able to help. He took down my number because he was about to leave with his wife for a well-baby checkup with their pediatrician. I thanked him for the lovely conversation about children, and even though I had only just met him, I could hear the compassion in his voice about Gerard's disability.

I hung up the phone wondering what to do next. Before I could make my next move, the phone rang. It was Mike, and his voice sounded a little apprehensive. All I remember was him asking me, "Who the hell are you, Mrs. Nabet?" I had no idea what he was talking about. He went on to explain that when he hung up the phone, he heard a voice telling him to "go and help" me. It frightened him. He then put his wife on the phone, and she told me that they were not religious but my story about Gerard touched them. She could not explain what had just happened to her husband. All she knew was that he was not going with her to the pediatrician. When Mike got back on the phone, he said he was going to help me and was en route to my home!

Forty-five minutes later, Mike arrived with a huge dump truck and a trailer carrying a very large backhoe. When he got to my driveway, he realized that there was a large branch from one of our trees blocking his entrance to the yard. My husband came out to help, but Mike would not let my husband help in anyway. Mike just kept looking over at me and asking my husband, "Who is she?" We all still laugh at this.

Finally, I explained to Mike how God works: I know that those things the world thinks are impossible can become the possible with God's help. Nothing is impossible with God. When I asked for help and there was no help to be found, God and Mary provided. They moved all the obstacles out of the way until there was a clear path. This path is always straight and direct, and your personal guide is the Creator of the universe. Left to our own devices, we make turns and missteps that make us feel like we are falling off the track. But God, our loving Father, gently moves his hand to guide us back. I have fallen off the track so many times that it is a wonder that God did not give me a good shove instead of a gentle push. People always say that it is good to "have friends in high places," so why not make your *best friends* in the *highest* places?

Mike not only cut down most of my tree but also dug out enough dirt from my yard to enable us to have an in-ground pool! He even returned two days later with his brother to see if they could do anything else for me. Ed and our neighbors, Fred and Anthony, continued digging out my yard where Mike left off. Anthony would not stop working on the project until that pool was installed.

On the day of the pool installation, I had to go to the bank to get money to pay the installers. Thinking that Gerard would not miss me for that brief errand, I left my neighbor Katie at home with him. At that time, there were no cell phones, so there was no way for anyone to reach me. During my fifteen-minute absence, Gerard had a severe tantrum: he kicked his foot against the side of the house so hard that afterward he could not bear weight on his foot. I thought it was a possible hairline fracture, so Ed and I had to go with Gerard to the ER. This meant we had to leave Fred and Anthony with the installers to finish the remaining digging. I can still see Fred watching all the work as the "foreman" and Anthony, in his shorts, helping out with his fireman boots on.

We felt terrible leaving everyone at our home working while we took Gerard to the hospital. Ed had to drive because I could not handle Gerard by myself. We did not realize that we were in for quite an experience.

At the hospital, we had to put Gerard in a wheelchair because he could not even stand on his foot without screaming. My husband stayed with Gerard in an outer hallway as I went to have Gerard registered. The nurse in triage was not aware that Gerard was significantly autistic, so when she told me to wheel him into the triage booth to take his vital signs, I knew that would be a bad idea. I told her that Gerard was so scared that he was starting to flip out in the hallway.

When word passed that I was in the hallway with Gerard, several of my ER friends came out to see me. Seeing Gerard with such fear and agitation literally brought tears to their eyes. They did not know how to help me, but their love and support was more help than they ever could have imagined. They served me with their love, something we all need to learn and practice in our lives. My friends in the ER always make me feel like I am still one of them. They greeted me with hugs and kisses, and they are truly my extended family. Thankful for this blessing, I always keep the ER staff in my prayers and thoughts.

This ER is at a major hospital on Long Island, so it is quite large. The nurses made room for Gerard in one of the isolation rooms which is a closed unit with a door. In order to get to this room, we had to wheel Gerard through the middle of the ER! By this time, Gerard was terrified, and he was wringing his hands at a very rapid pace. He kept repeating, "No doctor," at least three hundred times. Though it was not unusual for him to repeat words for hours on end, he said these words very rapidly with much urgency.

When I opened the main doors to wheel him in, he went crazy. He screamed at such a high pitch that patients in the surrounding beds were first startled and then alarmed. To make matters worse, Gerard stiffened his legs, making it impossible to push the wheelchair. My husband had to position the chair way back so that it was doing a "wheelie" to get it through.

Thank God Gerard calmed down when we got him into the isolation room. The ER physician came in with a look on his face that I will never forget. I could see all the sorrow and compassion he had for all of us. The doctor realized that Gerard could not be X-rayed without sedation, so he had to find a drug suitable for Gerard. There are certain types of sedatives that have reverse effects with autistic children. One drug might tranquilize a normal child but have the effect of hyperexcitability on an autistic one.

Gerard would not even let the doctor *touch* his foot. In the interim, I made Gerard try to stand on his foot with no luck. The doctor was willing to try anything that I suggested. We tried one oral medication with no result; Gerard would not even take a sip after smelling it. Intravenous medication was the next choice, but the thought of holding Gerard down for an IV was enough to make me sick.

Things were looking hopeless, and I prayed for Jesus to make Gerard's foot well. After a few minutes, I happened to notice Gerard moving his ankle and foot when he could not move them at all before without screaming. Because Gerard has always trusted me, he allowed me to rotate his foot by his ankle. He did not make a sound. I asked him to stand up, and he stood up, putting his full weight on the foot with no apparent pain or discomfort. I then proceeded to make him walk in the small cubicle, and Gerard walked on the foot as if nothing had ever happened to it!

I remember looking at my husband and not being able to speak. Just a few minutes before, Gerard could not even slightly bend his foot, and now he was standing with no pain at all. I went and told the doctor, who was very happy with the outcome.

As we were leaving, God gave me one more gift: Gerard left on foot with no screaming or tantrum. My friends were all together by the nurses' station and had the same look that I saw on the doctor's face. Sometimes I think that God allows other people to see what autism is like so that they have a better understanding of what you go through as a family. One of the hardest things about living with autism is that other people cannot really imagine it. You try to explain it until you are blue in the face, and many people still cannot understand. It is both mentally and emotionally painful when you have to describe your child's disorder or behavior to someone who is showing little or no tolerance for your child. Thank God these unkind people are few. Most people try to understand, even if they cannot fully imagine how different your life is compared to theirs.

When we finally got home from the ER, our pool had been installed, and there were three hoses running to fill it up. One was from our home, one was from our next-door neighbors Lorraine and Frank, and one was from Katie and Fred's home. If Joan and Anthony's hose could reach our yard, their hose would have been there too! When I saw the hoses filling the completed pool, I thanked God and Mother Mary for sending us these wonderful neighbors. I am doubly blessed in that my neighbors are very receptive to my religious views. It is a true blessing to be able to mention or thank God in front of people without feeling uncomfortable or embarrassed.

I called each of the neighbors to thank them, and then I called the ER and thanked the physician and the nurses who had been so kind to Gerard. They will never know how much it meant to me as a parent that they showed such kindness and compassion. Now every time I am in the pool, I think of Mike and all the people who helped us make it possible for Gerard to truly enjoy the summer as God had intended him to.

CHAPTER 15

The Good Neighbors

Blessings come in many forms. One of these blessings is having good neighbors. When you have wonderful neighbors like ours, you are very blessed indeed. Next door to us live Frank and Lorraine, who are very kind and sweet. They are an elderly couple who never had children. Lorraine always prays for Gerard and our family, and they never complain when they hear Gerard acting out with loud screams or tantrums.

On the other side of Frank and Lorraine, there is the home of Katie and her husband, Fred. They have two sons: Fred and Patrick (who is my Eddie's best friend). Katie and her kids are frequent visitors to my home. Other than my immediate family, Katie and her sons have experienced more of Gerard's behavior than anyone else.

Katie has been a wonderful friend to me, and we have reached a level of friendship where I never have to make excuses about anything to her. When the children were little, Katie would come early to my house with her son Patrick so all the boys could wait for the bus in the morning. Some mornings, it would take me over *one and a half hours* just to get Gerard ready for school! He would be throwing a tantrum and screaming while the house looked like they dropped an atomic bomb in the middle of my living room! Every toy we had was out or on the floor to try to distract Gerard. But the only person who was distracted was *me*! Katie took this all in stride; she would just pitch in and ask me what I wanted her to do. I laugh when I think back to all she did for me. Half the time, she would be making a jelly sandwich in the kitchen or helping me to get Gerard dressed. She would stay for over an hour, helping me even though she worked full-time as a nurse in a doctor's office. Her true friendship was apparent during those early days when most people would have run from our home.

Katie's deep compassion for Gerard came from her own need for compassion. Her son Fred had a learning disability, requiring a lot of time and effort to help him with his lessons. Katie was also raised a Catholic and knew about Mother Mary, but Katie did not really know Mother Mary as she does now. Once when Katie was feeling very down, I told her to visit the statue of Mother Mary at the local church and tell all her pain and sorrows, struggles and hardships. Mother Mary, in turn, will bring them to her Son, who will know exactly what to do with them. I gave Katie this advice when Fred was five years old, and, by carrying the cross of Fred's disability, Katie has come to know our heavenly mother. Fred is now in the tenth grade and doing very well.

If I had to pinpoint why my friendship with Katie is so good after so many years, I would have to say it is because of our humor. Katie is very funny, and we laugh at the same things. We make it a point to laugh often—which is a necessity to survive in this world. It took Katie a while to laugh when I would make a joke about autism and Gerard. It was not until she realized that it was a release for me to make "light" of a serious situation that she could joke also.

For example, there was one time when we were talking on the driveway that Gerard shut my back door and locked me out! Katie looked like she was going to be sick. I told her not to panic; I thought I could get Gerard to open the door by bribing him with an ice cream cone. There we were, looking in my front kitchen window, asking Gerard to open the door. Of course, he just stood there with that avoidance gaze. So I brought out the "big guns" and asked him if he would like an ice cream cone. Gerard kept saying yes, but he would not go to open the door! It was so funny as we watched, helplessly, from the window as Gerard proceeded to pull a chair over to the refrigerator and get out the ice cream. Then he moved the chair over to the closet to get the cones. By the time he opened the cabinet drawer to get the spoon, I was yelling at him to "Stop being autistic, and open the door for Mommy!" Katie gave me with a strange look, and then we burst out laughing. It broke the tension, and we agreed that you must find the humor in it, or you will crack up! Gerard continued to get everything ready for the ice cream cone, and then he opened the door. Looking back now, I realize how very *bright* he was to have done all those steps at that time.

Even though Katie does not live with autism, she understands it very well from all the time she has spent in our home. Over time, Katie has also become a witness to many miraculous things that have happened in my life that could not be easily explained. She has never been surprised by the outcome of these events, because I always remind her of God and Mother Mary's intercession. This special friendship with Katie is a true gift from God and Mother Mary, who knew that we needed each other to carry our crosses together. I value Katie's friendship more than she will ever know, and we love each other very much. We have laughed quite a bit and have cried with each other. With Katie, I have been blessed with a "fifth" sister.

My main wish for Katie is to help her get rid of her "baggage." She lugs around all these extra burdens that she chooses to carry. Sometimes, she goes from baggage to "steamer trunks." When she reaches the steamer-trunk level, it is very obvious: she goes into overdrive to get her son Fred through midterms or finals. She should be known as "the flash card queen" because over the years, she has made thousands. This does not include all the tapes she has made so that Fred can absorb his lessons through auditory material. This woman has worked harder than anyone could expect to make her son the best that he can be. However, as we have gotten older, we realize now that it has always been in God's hands; we just did not want to give up "the controls."

I remind Katie constantly that her son Fred is in God's hands, but every year, she cannot help but worry about the same issues: Fred is having a difficult time in school, or he is distracted. Her worries intensify around the holidays and during the spring—but these are the same times that so-called "normal kids" have difficulty paying attention too! She laughs when I remind her that her story sounds "so familiar." In my prayers, I wish that she would totally surrender her son Fred over to God so she would have more time to enjoy life instead of using all that energy to worry and try to predict the outcome of what God has already prepared. Fred always ends up doing very well.

We have been neighbors for seventeen years, and our children have grown up together as well. We have shared plenty of wonderful memories for our "internal scrapbook." One of my favorites is Halloween when Katie and I, along with the kids and our husbands, would go trick-or-treating. Ed always takes that day off so that he does not miss out on all the fun. Years ago, he would wear a mask or something funny as we followed the same route year after year. We have to follow the exact same route because Gerard is with us, and *God forbid* you try to change that routine! Gerard does not care if it is a torrential rain! We still have to go the *exact same route* that we have followed for the past ten years. By the time we get home, we are exhausted. By tradition, Katie, Fred, and the kids have dinner at our house where I always make a big Italian dinner. My mom usually puts it in the oven about an hour before we get home so that it is warm and ready for us. Katie always brings great desserts, and there is a nice bottle of chilled wine. Halloween is always a very special memory because it is filled with much love and joy about wonderful friendships.

Halloween also reminds me of my very sincere friendship with Katie. Even though Katie's kids have gotten older and no longer need adult supervision to trick-or-treat, Katie always accompanies me when I take Gerard trick-or-treating. It is a constant that I never wonder about. If the tables were turned, Katie knows that I would be trick-or-treating with her until I was old and gray.

What is most special about my friendship with Katie is that she has always accepted what I have told her about my faith. Others may think that I am a little "off-the-wall" between my frequent references to God and Mother Mary and the strange events that have occurred in my life, but Katie accepts them all and sincerely believes in what

I have told her. Katie does not need to *see* before she *believes*. This is a wonderful trait, and her trust is the foundation of our friendship.

Likewise, I have a wonderful relationship with Katie's husband, Fred, who likes to joke around with me. He is a big fan of the New York Mets, while our home is a New York Yankees' "Bronx Bombers" household. I tell him that between our two homes is the "Mason-Dixon line" of baseball. Throughout the years as neighbors, I would always drop a seed about God and Mother Mary to Fred. He would always chuckle when I told him that God was "taking care of everything" for my Yankees. Fred tries his hardest to get me going during the Subway Series. When these two teams play against each other, Fred will call me from work, asking me to "knock off the Hail Marys for those Bronx Bombers." I laugh and then say another Hail Mary for them. Then I call Katie up and tell her to tell Fred to "stop bothering me from work," and we all laugh about it.

Katie and Fred's younger son is Patrick, whom we have nicknamed "Patty-Pops." Patrick is turning fourteen this year and has reached a very sensitive age. Although Katie often tells me how "fresh" Patrick is getting, I never pay any attention, because I have already seen special things in Patrick. When Patrick was young, he played in my home and always had a sincere love for Gerard. During those early years, Gerard threw tantrums frequently, but Patrick always remained kind and sweet to him. There were times when Patrick took some really hard pinches or shoves, yet he still came back enthusiastically to play with Gerard. I have reminded Katie about this many times and told her that nothing she says about Patrick will ever change my mind about him.

Once, my son Eddie had to go on a class trip in the fifth grade for five days. In the back of my mind, I was a little scared wondering how I was going to get through the week not knowing how to play Gerard's video games! But God took care of this when Patrick made himself available to me. I had to call him twice. There, in my son's absence, Patrick did his best to fill his friend's shoes. Patrick stayed with Gerard in the playroom for quite some time. To this day, Patrick always seeks out my sons Gerard and Joseph for a hug and kiss. Gerard completely trusts Patrick and sees what I see in him: the love of God that opens Patrick's heart to a disabled child. This is a rare characteristic to find in young people today.

Both Patrick and his brother, Fred, possess this gift of love and compassion. Fred volunteers by cooking at a local home that supplies housing and meals to families of children from out of town who are receiving medical care. When I recently asked Fred if he liked volunteering, he responded that it made him "feel really good inside." That special feeling cannot be purchased in a store: it only comes when you totally open your heart to God's will.

God has blessed us with many good kids on our block and the surrounding blocks. One neighbor, down at the end of the block, is Thomas, who also has great compassion for Gerard. Thomas has had his own cross to bear: he was diagnosed with juvenile diabetes a few years ago. It must be very difficult for a child to handle such a demanding disease, but his parents have been very supportive while going through their own pain and fear.

Eddie also plays with a large group of friends that we call "The Rope Lane Kids." This is a wonderful group of boys who have grown up together. They all come to play baseball in the summer and football in the winter at the park across the street. In the summer, there might be twelve to fourteen boys in my home! Who needs camp? They are all good boys with special gifts and talents, and all of them acknowledge Gerard by having him "slap me five." It is very moving for Eddie to see his friends accept his brother for who he is. There is never embarrassment or shame, only an outpouring of love. In my heart, I know my block receives these many blessings from Our Lord and Mother Mary because of Gerard. We have all come to understand the way of the cross from knowing Gerard.

Next to Katie and Fred are our neighbors Joan and Anthony. They were blessed with five children. Anthony was a New York City fireman who was filled with enough life for ten men. Anthony was willing to help everyone with everything and was known as the "mayor" of our block. He was the kind of man who would literally "drop everything" to help a friend or someone in need. He would "give you the shirt off his back" if you asked. If I needed something for Gerard, I knew I could count on Anthony for help. Anthony liked to joke with me, but he always admired my faith and believed that I "lived out my faith in actions." Little did we all know that in a few years a tremendous cross would be given to them as a family. The outcome, however, would be a blessing, and Anthony would teach all of us how to reach a deeper level of trust in God and his will.

Joan and Anthony were very social and always entertaining people. Both of them came from large Italian families who gathered often for birthday parties and holidays. Every Sunday, we would see Joan and Anthony drive by our home en route to a party or gathering of some kind. Their van was filled with kids, and they would wave and honk their horn at us. It was not until much later that Joan confessed that she and Anthony sometimes felt uncomfortable going out so much on weekends when they knew my family had to stay home a lot because of Gerard's autism. It is true that sometimes when they drove past, I wondered where they were going. I would then "daydream" about going to family gatherings and parties without having to do lots of preparation and problem-solving. Sometimes, it would make me feel melancholy and blue. During those times, God gave me the strength to go on, and I became determined that one day God would help Gerard enough so that we also could go out to social events.

It has taken many years, but that dream has been fulfilled. Gerard now loves going out to social events. He still needs constant supervision, but, as a family, we are able to do more than we did before. There are still some types of events that we cannot attend, but I believe that God will eventually help make those possible too. It is patience that is the hardest lesson to master. Once one learns patience, life takes on a whole new meaning. Now when my family goes out, we all make the most of it!

On the other side of Joan and Anthony's house is the home of my friend Jenny and her sons, James and Paul. Her boys always played with mine when they were young. Jenny was divorced and raising the boys on her own. This is a difficult cross in itself, but Jenny is a woman of great faith and devotion to Mother Mary. I always say, "You have to go through the bad stuff to get to the good stuff," and that is what happened to Jenny; she went through a difficult situation but trusted in God's will. In return, she met a wonderful man whom she eventually married. Ed and I had a wonderful time at her wedding because it was truly happy, filled with joy, and blessed with God's peace.

Most people think they are blessed if they have one good neighbor. Think of how lucky I am to have a block-load!

CHAPTER 16

More Gifts

Soon after our pool was installed, I started working in the backyard to try to get the rest of the yard in order. We had a very large mound of dirt in our yard from the backhoe's digging of the pool. Picture a lovely new above-ground pool surrounded by a five-foot-high mound of dirt everywhere! Only a quarter of the backyard still had grass, and it was *not* near the pool, so there was dirt and mud all over the house whenever anyone went swimming. My husband and I knew that we could not possibly level the remaining dirt by ourselves because the mound was too high. We also needed grass to keep the dirt and mud from going everywhere. It was hard trying to keep the pool clean and prevent the kids from tracking all the mud on their feet into the house!

The big dilemma was that our funds were "low," but the amount of work was "high." Once again, I needed to summon divine intervention. During all the years I have been married, I have been amazed at how the Lord has always provided for us. Financially, my husband is employed in a civil service job that has great benefits but only average pay. We have always lived from paycheck to paycheck, never knowing what bills another week may bring. So it has become a common practice for me to bring all my needs and bills to God. *I never beg.* Instead I go like a "business manager" and lay out all our bills before him. Through prayer, I tell God that these are the bills and this is our income. The bills are always higher than the income, but God always provides what we have most needed. For instance, Gerard's disorder brings its own set of unusual bills; between pizza and the local fast-food restaurant, I spend about sixty dollars extra a week for Gerard in addition to my normal food shopping. Somehow, there is enough money for these expenses, and I believe God provides for us because of our deep and sincere trust in him.

My husband guessed that there was $400 left in our budget after the pool was installed. We called several landscapers for estimates to level the dirt in the yard. All their estimates were well over $400! My sister-in-law then told us that she had a neighbor who worked for a major construction-vehicle sales company. He was willing to come and do the job, but he wanted $300 an hour. She told us that he was a perfectionist and would do an excellent job, but he was also "strictly business" and let people know his fee before doing a job—even for his neighbors.

After discussing this with my husband, we decided to let him come for one hour's worth of work. We hoped that he could just level the huge mound of dirt. Then my husband and I could rake it until it was level, even if that took the rest of the summer. God and Mother Mary knew that Gerard was already a big job by himself, and they wanted us to enjoy the pool that we had worked so hard to get. So once again, after many struggles, they gave us a blessing.

My sister-in-law's neighbor arrived with a Bobcat for leveling the dirt on a trailer. The man met Gerard who was home that day. Thinking that it might take only an hour with the machinery, I explained to the man that I only wanted the dirt leveled on the large mound. I then left the man to his work. This man worked diligently for three hours, leveling my entire backyard! He reduced the area that sloped and made it much easier to manage. What he did not know was that I was in the house having a coronary wondering how in God's name I would ever be able to pay him! We did not have a savings account, so I could not just run to the bank to withdraw money, and there were no credit cards to take a cash advance. So I did what I have done a thousand times before: I prayed. I could hear my sister-in-law telling me that her neighbor *never* made exceptions to anyone about his fee. The longer I heard his machinery running outside, the more I felt palpitations in my chest.

Finally, the motor stopped, and I was faced with the inevitable: I owed him $900, and all I had was $400! You are probably wondering why I did not stop him after an hour. I can only say that I had a feeling that I was not supposed to *disturb* him. My husband kept telling me to go stop him, but something within my heart told me to let him finish. All I had to offer him, besides the money, was a picture of Mother Mary of Medjugorje.

This picture is of the statue that is present in Medjugorje, Yugoslavia. There have been apparitions of Mother Mary there since 1980. An apparition is an actual sighting or vision of Mother Mary, a saint, or even God to a human being. Most people are familiar with the apparitions of Fatima, Lourdes, and Guadalupe. But these are just a few of the many that occur throughout the world. My mom and Aunt Irene, along with three of my sisters, have made pilgrimages to Medjugorje; and the results of their pilgrimages have been very fruitful. Although I have never been there myself, my faith and devotion to Mary tell me that these are true visions. The pictures I have were blessed on the altar in Medjugorje where the apparitions occur.

The picture that I hand out also has a special prayer and blessing that goes to anyone who receives the picture. It is the *faith* behind the picture that allows Mary to intercede for you in heaven. My aunt's friend made up thousands of these pictures, had them blessed, and hands them out as part of her ministry of spreading the message of Medjugorje. My ministry is to hand out these pictures to whomever Mother Mary calls me to give one. Mother Mary inspires me to give out this special gift where it is needed. Although I have never been to Medjugorje, I believe in the apparitions and messages that Mother Mary gives there. Words cannot describe what Mother Mary has done for me as a woman and mother of a special child; she has taught me so many beautiful lessons through prayer that I am very proud to call her my "heavenly mother."

As I headed to the backyard, I was struck by another thought: what if this man was not a Catholic? Would he understand that the picture with a prayer on the back comes with a special blessing? When I finally reached him, I looked at the job he had done on my yard. It was done beautifully *and* professionally. The change caught me by surprise. Just three hours before, there was only a huge mound of dirt!

The man asked me if I was pleased with his work. I told him I was not only pleased but all the effort he put into this job brought tears to my eyes. Of course, you know what the next conversation topic would be: how much do I owe you? What I did not expect was what he said next: "Was *a hundred dollars* too much?" I thought he was teasing me, so I started to laugh nervously. I really wanted to hide and cry, but instead I was laughing at something that was not funny at all. When I finally stopped laughing, I realized that he was quite serious. He explained that his younger son had learning disabilities, which included speech delay when he was a toddler. Apparently, the man and his wife had gone through a difficult time, so he saw my family through compassionate and empathetic eyes.

I insisted that he take the $400, but he would not hear of it. He took the picture of Mother Mary with tearful eyes and thanked me even though he was Lutheran, and not Catholic. This just shows me that mankind has made different sects and religions, but we are all under one God, and Mary is the mother of us all—not just Catholics. I cannot tell you how much thanks and praise went to God and Mary for sending this man to me. He may have left with $100 and a picture of Mother Mary, but he also made a friend who would pray for him and his family always.

Now the ground was level, but it was all dirt. To plant grass seed for the lawn would take at least three weeks for germination and growth. By that time, I would be tearing my hair out, trying to keep the house and pool clean. I went to yellow pages and called some nurseries for prices on sod. Most of the nurseries had already sold out their supply for the summer. I finally found one local nursery that could get me what I needed. My husband and I had no idea what sod cost, but when we gave them our measurements, the price they quoted for the sod, and its delivery was *$300!*—exactly what we had left! Our sod was soon delivered, and my husband and I laid it all out on a hot July day.

This whole episode showed me once again that nothing is impossible with God's help. Our trust in God moved obstacles out of the way and completed what needed to be finished. In the process, a new friend was made, and an introduction to Mother Mary was given. It was the best $400 I have ever spent. This was another one of the multiple blessings that have come to us from taking care of Gerard and saying yes to God. God never ceases to amaze me in the gifts and blessings he sends. Each event or gift is sent with the sincerest love, which just takes my breath away.

Our yard was finished, and we were enjoying our pool in so many ways. Gerard, like my other children, is a very strong swimmer. I sometimes think Gerard has some "dolphin genes" in him; he does this unusual underwater movement with his back to the floor of the pool and his belly up. He keeps his feet together and literally moves like a dolphin. The pool helps reduce a lot of Gerard's hyperactivity because he is able to swim for hours. It was also a great form of exercise for Gerard, who is generally not as physically active as the other kids. The pool has also been a surprise blessing for me. Each night after dinner, I go in the pool by myself for about twenty minutes before the rest of the family joins me. Those twenty minutes alone are probably the best part of my summer. I love the water, and I know that God also gave me this pool as a gift to help reduce my stress and anxiety. I always feel rejuvenated after getting out of the water. We have all been blessed with so many wonderful, funny memories of times in the pool.

The pool also provided entertainment for Gerard and the kids during those early years when times were very difficult. Because Gerard's various behaviors are often difficult to manage, it was often easier to just stay home. I cannot tell you how many parties or events we had to leave abruptly because of Gerard's behavior. Some people understood, but others did not, and it confused me that people would get upset if you had to leave early because of Gerard's situation. Did they think we planned his outbursts? Did they not see the pain and suffering we were going through at that moment? Those of you who come into contact with the parents or caretakers of autistic children, try to be compassionate and understand their discomfort.

There were many family parties we had to miss, and I remember sitting outside, daydreaming of what my sisters were doing or what they were talking about. It would bring tears to my eyes— not tears of jealousy but tears of loneliness and melancholy. At those times, I would pray to God to help me with the pain of loneliness. I offered all my pain up to God so that one day I could appreciate all the things that I had missed. What got me through those sad times was the hope that Gerard would improve as he got older. Hope is our most powerful ally.

Gerard has improved since those early years, and we can now go to events and places that were impossible before. We cannot go everywhere, but we are much freer and happier than before. When we cannot attend a party or event, I make a point of doing something special at home with the kids, so they never blame Gerard. They have all learned to "sacrifice with love."

CHAPTER 17

Danger Averted

Another blessing came to us that summer. We have a big metal shack in our yard where my husband stores all the yard tools. Ed happened to be cleaning out the shed one day and threw an old pool ladder behind the shed where there was a large tree (thirty to forty feet high). While Ed was busy cleaning, Gerard climbed the old ladder. Something told me to go out and check on Gerard. It must have been Gerard's guardian angel, because I suddenly saw Gerard on top of the shed and about to grab the electrical wires that ran from the main electrical pole! I screamed so loud that I caused Gerard to stop dead in his tracks.

My husband ran out of the shed to help me. In my instant prayer, I *demanded* God to send angels to get Gerard to turn around and come down—and that is just what happened! Gerard looked the same way he had when he was in the hospital for the CAT scan. Almost in a trance, Gerard kept saying, "Tarzan." He must have thought he could swing on those "vines," which were really the electric line. We later discovered that Gerard had moved the pool ladder against the tree, climbed up to a certain level in the tree, and then shimmied out onto the shed roof. I looked at my husband, and we said at the same time, "The tree has to come down."

Once again, I turned to the yellow pages looking for a tree surgeon this time. They could not give me an estimate over the phone but told me a tree of that size could cost over $600. We did *not* have $600! So I started praying. Just then my husband came in and told me that the electric company might be able to help us because a lot of the big branches were tangled around the electrical wires. I then called the electric company, and a lovely woman took down my information and set up an appointment for the following day with a field supervisor. She informed me that the tree might not need to be removed, but they could prune the big branches.

The following day, the field supervisor came to see the tree. I explained that Gerard was autistic and that once Gerard had gotten up there, there would be no stopping him from trying again. Even if Gerard did not actually go there again, he would drive me crazy trying to. Fortunately, God always sends me people who understand my situation. The field supervisor said I did not have to convince him: his neighbor's child was autistic. The field supervisor was very sympathetic to our situation. Although there was normally a six-week wait for tree removal, he bumped us to the top of the list. A crew would arrive the following day, and there would be no charge for the service. After setting up the date and time, the field supervisor reviewed with me what would be done: they would cut down all the branches and leave the tree stump at nine feet high. The branches and debris would be our own responsibility to remove. This seemed more than fair to me since I was relieved that they could remove something that might be very dangerous to Gerard.

The next morning, a two-man crew arrived. I was getting Gerard bathed for summer school, and they watched as Gerard got onto the school bus. When I offered them something to drink, I told them about what happened with the tree days earlier and also about Gerard's condition. One of the men asked me about Gerard's neurologist. Apparently, this man's son had suffered from attention deficit disorder. I could easily see how upset this father was because his son felt stupid and was hanging out with the wrong crowd because he did not fit in. I told the man that I would pray for his son and also gave him the name of Gerard's doctor. The man was very appreciative, and as they went off to work, they confirmed what the supervisor had told me about the service to be rendered.

I had a pediatrician's appointment that day for Eddie's physical, and I could not cancel. You cancel one of those appointments, and you cannot get another one for the whole summer! Because it was a hot summer day, I left a cooler with ice and cold cans of soda outside for the men. As I was leaving, the backyard became filled with branches, logs, and debris everywhere; and I knew my husband, and I would be busy for hours that evening. Even though I was thrilled about having the tree pruned, the thought of the cleanup made me tired just thinking about it. I left each man a money tip and a picture of Mother Mary of Medjugorje; everyone who does work that assists in something for Gerard receives a picture. This picture was especially welcome to the tree cutter with the teenage son. There was so much stress and anxiety in his face, and pain in his voice. It is not hard to recognize these signs in others when you have experienced them so much yourself.

Upon leaving, I thanked them with all my heart and wished them the best. They told me that I needed to notify the phone, cable, and electric companies to come and tighten the wires that ran from the pole to my home. The heavy branches from the tree had weighed the wires down, causing them to stretch and loosen across the shed roof. I then promised to call all three utilities to take care of the loose wires.

On the way home from the pediatrician, I could not help thinking about all the hard yard work that lay ahead. My husband would not be home for several hours, so I thought I might try to clean up as much as I could before he got home. My daughter, Chrissy, had come along for the ride and was teasing me about how much work it would be. When I pulled up to our house, I saw *no debris at all!* At first, I thought the men had closed the fence leading to the back-yard to contain everything. But when I entered the backyard, it was thoroughly clean. There was not even *a leaf* left on the lawn! I went behind the shed, expecting to see the nine-foot tree stump. Instead, there was nothing! Not only was the tree removed, but they had even *ground* the stump for me!

I looked around in utter amazement at this most kind and generous act. When I returned to the house to call my husband, I noticed a note taped to the back door. It was from the father of the teenager; not only had they removed the entire tree for me, but they had even tightened all the wires to my home so that I did not need to call the utilities! The note went on to explain that after I left, they got a little spooked. They said that when they saw Gerard that morning, they had a strange feeling. Not a bad feeling, but a feeling that they were going to do a complete removal and cleanup. What struck me as miraculous was that each of the men had this same feeling when they pulled up to the home, but neither one confided in the other until I left for the pediatrician's office.

Do I think this was just chance or a coincidence? *Absolutely not.* When God wants something done, he moves *everything* out of the way and allows for the free flow of his gifts and graces. I always tell people that God has done these wondrous things in my life because I have been receptive to his love and friendship. God wants to share these gifts with *everyone.* All you have to do is open your heart to God. Once your heart is open, his wonders start to unfold. All your relationships become blessed and more intimate and loving. I know I do not want to live a second of my life without a sharing, loving, and nurturing relationship with God and Mother Mary.

The reason I think that many strangers have been so kind and generous in response to Gerard's autism is that they are inspired by God. God knows how much work it takes to raise a child with a disability—much more than with a normal child. Because this work is so difficult, God inspires those around you to see through compassionate eyes and help you carry your cross.

My neighbors, Katie and Fred, came to see the grinded stump, the note, and the clean yard. Fred laughed, saying, "Only at your house Liz!" and Katie said, "It doesn't surprise me. Not coming from this house, it doesn't." In my prayers, I thanked God for sending me these two wonderful men from the electric company. To this day, I still pray for the tree cutter's son and for both their families.

When God bestows gifts and blessings, it is always important to remember to *thank him.* After all, don't we all like to be thanked when we offer a gift? Why would it be any different for God? We teach our children to thank people who give them something or treat them with kindness. If a child is appreciative and loving, you want to do more for him or her because of his or her great heart. But a child who demands things because he or she expects them or feels it is your duty to provide, then the last thing you want to do is give them more. It is the *same* with God. The more you praise him with a thankful heart, the more he wants to send you. We have all prayed at one time or another for something from God. How many times have we received the gift without returning a simple acknowledgment of gratitude?

I learned the habit of giving thanks from a very early age. My mom reminded us daily of all the things we should be thankful for. When you make a conscious effort to give thanks, it becomes a wonderful tradition. Simple gifts take on a new light when they are seen through thankful eyes. I have learned to give thanks for everything that comes my way, even the difficulties and the problems because I know that they all have a purpose in my life. If it had not been for Gerard's autism, I would have missed the joy of thankfulness, which leads to a more peaceful and contented life. So I give great thanks every day to God for blessing me with Gerard.

CHAPTER 18

A Visitation

Another unexpected gift came when we were on vacation in Orlando, Florida. The major theme parks in Florida are Gerard's favorites, but going on vacation is a major undertaking for our family. The physical preparations alone are overwhelming. When you combine the physical process with the mental preparation, you are totally exhausted before you have even stepped out the door! Each trip must be planned out thoroughly from beginning to end. There is no such a thing as just "packing up and going" with autism.

We always have to travel by car because I never know how Gerard will react. I certainly do not need him to have a tantrum at thirty-five thousand feet in an airplane! With our luck, they would land the plane immediately and ask us to leave. That would be a *too* intense an experience for any of us. Believe it or not, Gerard is actually very good in the car. He loves going out, so he does not mind a long car ride. As long as he has his "stuff" with him, he is fine. By "stuff," I mean all the things needed to keep your autistic child calm and busy. These things give Gerard a sense of security by having "something from home" with him.

We never tell Gerard beforehand that we are headed to Florida. Instead I tell him that we are going on a vacation to Maryland. This way he does not look for the big theme parks on the *first* day of our trip. It takes twenty-two hours to drive from our home to Orlando.

Once, I made the mistake of telling him we were going to Florida at the beginning of the trip. When we reached Savannah, Georgia, we decided to stop for the first night. Having driven sixteen hours, we were all exhausted but made it through dinner calmly. But when we got back to the hotel, Gerard flipped out. He wanted to be in Orlando *now!* His outburst was so bad that the hotel manager came to our room and asked, "Is everything all right?" I immediately began praying. I just kept saying one Hail Mary after another and asking Mary to calm Gerard and allow his sleep medication to take effect. Mother Mary has never let me down; Gerard did relax and fall asleep.

For parents and the family, those violent tantrums are the hardest times with autism. You feel utterly helpless. You cannot get through to your child, and it can be very overwhelming. Even after the tantrum passes, you are left with a feeling of frustration and sadness. I felt so overcome at times that I almost gave up trying new things or going to new places. It was much easier and safer to remain in the confines of my own home. But I was wrong; staying home only led to greater loneliness and isolation. When Gerard acts out now, I try to figure out what the trigger could be. I always pray for divine intervention, try to correct the situation if possible, and do the best that I can for that moment. God never fails to show me what Gerard needs.

I always make a detailed itinerary so that we can all have a really good vacation. Because Gerard has a photographic memory, he never forgets where things are located in the amusement parks. Some rides he loves so much that he makes us go on them several times. He loves roller coasters—the faster, the better! The most wonderful thing offered at the theme parks is the *handicapped pass*. This pass allows us to go on a ride without waiting on long lines. This is a lifesaver because Gerard has a very difficult time understanding the concept of waiting; he can become frustrated easily.

It is only within the last year and a half that Gerard has gained some awareness of the words: *wait, soon,* and *later.* I was able to teach him these concepts at home with help from the school and the use of visual aids. Visual aids for Gerard helped me so much in the early years. For example, we keep an itinerary of Gerard's week up on the refrigerator using Velcro. This way Gerard can *see* what is coming up for him next, and he is better able to transition from one thing to the next. With autism, we have had to learn a whole new "vocabulary" as we try to teach Gerard to master our language and vocabulary. Phrases like "quiet hands," "quiet feet," "good looking," and "good talking" have become a permanent part of our vocabulary.

On this particular trip to Florida, Gerard was seven years old. It was the last two weeks of August, and the theme parks were very crowded. We were at one of the movie theme parks and had gone on every ride several times until evening. There was one ride with a tower that Gerard, Eddie, and my husband took three times in a row! That would be enough times for most people, unless you're *Gerard*. I could not handle going on this ride, so my poor husband was stuck going a *fourth* time.

Toward the end of the evening, they had a final show with all the movie characters near the lagoon. We left the tower ride to get seats for the show. Gerard loved the show, and he would have been happy to sit there for *ten hours* if there had been a nonstop show. As with everything else, the show came to an end, and the crowd started to leave the outdoor theater.

We had Gerard in a wheelchair in the park because it was easier to manage him that way when we were all walking around. As I wheeled him out of the theater, he started to repeat the word *tower*. He started in a low voice and repeated what he was thinking over and over. Simultaneously, he began to wring his hands with each repetition of the word. This behavior is called *perseverating*. His word repetition then got progressively louder and louder. At that point, if his request is not met, he escalates into a full-blown tantrum.

In this particular tantrum, Gerard escalated faster than I was able to wheel him over to the tower ride so that he could see that it was closed. The whole park was shutting down, and the lane that led to the ride was already darkened. In front of the ride, the large iron gates were chained and locked, and the ride itself was completely dark. There was no one else in sight because everyone else was heading to the exits.

In this tantrum, Gerard was so out of control that I can still remember his screams. He would not get out of the wheelchair, and he would not let me push it further. He had his feet firmly planted on the ground in front of him. His screams escalated to the point where I thought people would think we were murdering him in this dark alley.

In this situation, we were helpless. As my husband became nervous, he began to pace and worry. Ed began saying, "We are *never* going to get Gerard out of this park!" There was nothing that I could do to calm or correct this situation. My husband stood at the entrance to the lane, pacing back and forth and muttering under his breath. My husband was as terrified as I was, and our helplessness caused panic and terror to set in because we saw no solution to this problem. I tried to keep myself from losing it altogether for Eddie's sake. Eddie was only eight and completely frightened. As scary as this was for parents, it was horrifying to a child.

Eddie was crying so hard for me to help Gerard, but I knew in my heart that there was nothing I could do to calm Gerard. Eddie finally looked at me, with tears running down his face, and told me that we needed *a miracle*. The moment he said it, I knew he was right! This would require a lot more help than I normally prayed for. I needed to pull out all the stops. Instead of begging, I looked up into the heavens and *demanded* that God send an *angel* to help me calm Gerard. I do not remember whether I got the last words out, but, out of nowhere, a man suddenly appeared in front of Gerard. He startled Eddie and me, because we did not see him approach. I did not even get to tell the man about Gerard's autism. The man just started talking to Gerard in a soft, low-toned voice. He knelt down by the side of the wheelchair and said that he had a "message" and called Gerard by his first name. The man said, "Gerard, the ride is finished for tonight. It is time to go home. You can come back tomorrow."

Gerard went from totally crazed to a completely calm state that reminded me of the incident with the CAT scan. Gerard put his feet back up on the wheelchair's footrests and allowed me to wheel him out. He was moaning as if he wanted to continue his tantrum but was being put on "pause."

Ed, Eddie, and I were in such shock that I cannot remember whether I thanked the man enough. I do remember saying that I had just demanded God to send me an angel to help calm my son. The man did not say a word to me. He just kept smiling. I turned around to have Ed and Eddie tell the story about how we asked for God's help. When we turned back to the man, he was gone! My husband looked like he had just seen a ghost, and he kept saying aloud, "Where did that guy come from?" Although Eddie was very young, he was not too young to notice that the man had used Gerard's name—even though none of us had spoken to him! Ed said there was no way that he could have missed seeing the man if the man had come up through the lane! We were each left with a sense of wonder and amazement. For Eddie, it was the fact that the man called Gerard by name without being introduced. For my husband, it was the fact that the man appeared without my husband seeing him pass by. My own sense of amazement came from the man's sudden appearance, his calming of Gerard, and his just as sudden disappearance!

Am I really surprised? No. As I have said before, everything is possible with God. I needed help right then and there, and help came. This is a blessing that comes to all children of God. We may wonder why we had to endure that horrible tantrum, but I do not think we will ever fully understand God's ways. It is by accepting autism, with all its difficult twists and turns, that we are allowed opportunities for spiritual growth. Although I believe I am a strong woman, God knows I need challenges to continue to grow and develop. Through events like these with autism, my whole family sees the power of prayer and the need for complete surrender to obtain God's help.

This tantrum had my family tossed about on the high seas, and we felt close to drowning, but God sent us this man who became not only our lifeboat but brought us safely to shore. Dear Angel, whoever you are, we thank you from the bottom of our hearts for your help. You have added to all the blessings that allow me to grow stronger in my faith.

We have not gone on vacation as a family since that trip, but God had other things planned for us during the next five years.

CHAPTER 19

A Wonder

Each day is a part of a great story in the making. With each problem, there is a solution from God, and his overall message is the same: to remain faithful and joyous, and to find humor and laughter in each day. Where there is God, there is hope; and since God is everywhere, then hope is everywhere too.

When the experimental drug Secretin was first introduced in the medical community, I was very anxious to see the televised documentary about it. My husband and I were glued to the television set because the documentary was quite impressive. It told the story of a mother and her family who may have accidentally come across a possible cure for autism. The only difference between her story and ours was that her son also had gastrointestinal disturbance. I absorbed every word of the panel of specialists in the documentary. My husband was so impressed that he wanted me to investigate it immediately. I even daydreamed about Gerard receiving a total cure from autism. I imagined Gerard completely well and saw us as a family doing everything that we had not been able to do because of Gerard's autism.

As in all other times of my life, I brought the matter to prayer. My prayer to God was that if Gerard was chosen to receive this experimental hormone, then God would bring the opportunity to us. After several weeks of prayer, I met a woman at Eddie's school who told me that there was going to be a pilot program using experimental injections of Secretin. She gave me the name of the neurologist leading the experiment. My hopes were confirmed when a close friend mentioned that she liked and used this same neurologist. Not sure what to expect, I called and made an appointment.

On my first visit, there was a woman in the waiting room with her son. The boy was a year younger than Gerard and was talking beautifully with great eye contact. Actually, when I saw this boy, I could not figure out why he was in a pediatric neurology office at all. I then "diagnosed" him in my mind as having febrile seizures or some seizure disorder.

When the mother of this child started talking to me, she asked questions about Gerard. She then told me that before Secretin, her son had been significantly autistic; he hardly ever made eye contact, and he basically did not speak. I thought I was *dreaming*, even though I was wide awake! She told me that her son was also in the pilot program for Secretin. After the first dose, her son literally "woke up" from autism, and by nightfall, he was talking and understanding what was going on around him. She also told me that her son's autism was originally worse than Gerard's. This was very hard to believe, but I found it a wonderful boost of hope.

Under the pilot program, Secretin was expensive, and the protocol was that Gerard had to receive it every six weeks. The medication had to be given through an IV injection, and the thought of that made me very anxious and nervous. How would we administer this drug to Gerard by IV when he would not even let my pediatrician listen to his heart by stethoscope! I knew that I had to surrender this worry to God. If Gerard was to receive this medication, God would have to find the way. I kept reminding myself that I needed to let God handle all the details and all would be well.

The neurologist conducted a thorough physical examination of Gerard. We also had to answer a multitude of questions before Gerard was accepted into the experiment. Once we were finished with the exam and the paperwork, the neurologist gave me a prescription for Secretin. There were only a small number of pharmacies that carried the drug, and each injection cost $250! This cost was not covered by insurance because the drug was still under FDA investigation.

My mom, Aunt Irene, my cousin Patty, and her friend Sister Patty contributed money to help pay for the prescription injections for Gerard. It was a very nerve-racking experience, and we had no idea what to expect. I prayed to accept whatever was God's will and promised God that if Gerard improved at all from Secretin, then I wanted God to send me another autistic child and their family to help. This way, I would never forget the disease that had such a huge impact on my life. But, as many people will tell you, be careful what you ask of God; he hears and answers *all* prayers.

The neurologist had ordered extensive blood work, an EEG, and an EKG on Gerard before we began the injections in order to show Gerard's baseline state. Because of Gerard's prior behavior, we were afraid to take him to the lab for the tests. Once, he had flipped out so much at the hospital that it took six adults to get him off the floor. How were we now going to get the preliminary tests done so that Gerard could receive Secretin?

God has always sent me truly good people to help me carry this cross of autism. My neighbor Katie knew how important this was to me. At the time, Katie was a nurse manager in a doctor's office (I had worked at the same office for a year, so I also knew the doctor). Katie brought home all the tubes that I needed for the blood work, and they even let me bring home an EKG machine so that I could try to get an EKG from Gerard.

It was a Monday morning, and I had been up since 4:00 a.m., contemplating how I could possibly draw blood from Gerard. He was like a wild animal in the hospital. What made me think he would be any different at home? I set up all the equipment and started to pray. *Every* saint was asked for help in this case. I then brought Gerard into my bedroom where I saw that he had that dazed, relaxed, trancelike look again. I promised to take him to our local toy store when we were finished. As he sat quietly, I took all the tubes of blood I needed from him for the tests. Then he lay down on the floor for the EKG, like a person who was in deep sleep, yet he was *wide awake*!

Later, reading the EKG, everyone was impressed that there were no "artifacts" in it. Artifacts are disturbances on an EKG or rhythm strip that are caused by the person's movement or other vibration.

Not even one artifact was noted, and Gerard's EKG was normal. Gerard's blood work was sent out to a lab from Katie's office, and it all came back in the normal range. How Gerard remained calm when his blood was drawn is still a mystery to me. My pediatrician could not believe that Gerard allowed me to do all these tests to him. Once again, I believe that divine intervention is the cause. God was trying to tell me from day one: "Lizzie move over, and let God take over!" God has been there for every step of my journey with my son. I was never alone even in those times when I *felt* abandoned and alone.

Gerard was now ready to receive Secretin. Everyone we knew was praying for Gerard on the day of his first injection. The neurologist was also able to introduce an IV butterfly for the injections, which made giving each injection to Gerard much easier. Gerard received his first dose of Secretin without any adverse reaction or side effects. Of course, I wanted to put him under a glass dome so that I could watch his every move and wait to hear his every word. I knew I had to be careful about getting my hopes up in case it did not work—or deep disappointment would follow.

The same night Gerard received Secretin, he came into the kitchen and verbally asked for a red ice pop. It was only *six hours* after the first injection! Eddie and I looked at each other and then ran to the freezer for the ice pop. We were on the phone all night telling everyone that Gerard had verbalized what he wanted for the first time. My joy that night was unbelievable, and my husband and kids were so excited.

The neurologist running the pilot program was thrilled. He had great enthusiasm and was anxious to hear if there were any positive or negative effects to the drug. His demeanor was always very compassionate toward Gerard, and he listened attentively to everything I told him about Gerard's response. Over these years, a special bond has developed between my family and this wonderful doctor.

Each day we saw more and more speech emerge, and there was a definite improvement with Gerard's cognitive ability. He would not be completely cured, but I saw definite improvement from his first dose of Secretin. His teachers also saw improvement in his schoolwork. The person who saw the greatest change in Gerard was my pediatrician, Dr. A——. This pediatrician has always been very kind to Gerard and my family, but he was also honest and objective in his findings about Gerard. Even he could not get over the difference in Gerard's behavior! Prior to Secretin therapy, Gerard would freak out in any doctor's office. Just having his ears or throat checked was a major ordeal. After Secretin, Gerard seemed to understand more and was able to handle situations much more calmly.

Although Gerard did not have a complete cure, he reached a plateau in which he was much more manageable at home and in the community. All our close friends and family saw a tremendous improvement in him.

There was one time when Gerard received Secretin, and it seemed to have no additional effect on him. My husband and I were very disappointed, but we later learned that Secretin does not work in the presence of antibiotics. Gerard had been on some antibiotics during this particular treatment, and I had forgotten to tell my neurologist at the time of injection.

In my heart, I knew that Gerard would not be completely healed by this drug. It was not in God's will. Instead Secretin improved Gerard's existing condition and life in a very positive way. Eventually, Gerard's neurologist had to stop his pilot program with Secretin when the FDA failed to approve the drug. Without the FDA approval, he could not administer any more Secretin. Fortunately, as a result of the Secretin therapy, Gerard's condition never regressed. All the good that Secretin provided stayed with Gerard and continues to benefit him to this day. I only wish that there had been a longer investigation into the effects of this drug on autistic children. Perhaps the children who did not show results had a different disorder than the children who showed positive results.

CHAPTER 20

A Promise Kept

I had promised God that if Gerard showed any results from the Secretin, God should send me a child with autism and family if they needed help. As I said before, watch what you ask for in prayer because all prayers are answered. They may not be answered in the way that we anticipate, but God knows what is best for us, and he answers the prayers in the best way.

Shortly after Gerard received his first dose of Secretin, I received a phone call from a nurse, with whom I was friendly, at Gerard's school. She asked if I knew anyone who could possibly help a woman with an autistic, blind thirteen-year-old daughter who needed to be watched in the mornings. The mother had to work and was not able to wait to put her daughter on the school bus. The father of this child had died several years earlier, so it was just the two of them. The child also had a seizure disorder that was controlled by medication.

I almost fell on the floor when I got this call because I had asked God to send this to me! When I told the nurse the story of how my prayer was answered, she said she had only called to see if I knew someone who could help. The child's previous babysitter was unable to continue because her husband was terminally ill and she had to turn all her attention to him. In my heart, I knew that this child was meant to come to me.

The next day, the mother, Jane, called to discuss the situation of her daughter, Mary. We talked for some time about both Gerard and Mary and the news about Secretin therapy. I could not imagine how hard it was for this single mother to raise a child with multiple handicaps on her own. It was hard enough for me to raise an autistic child in a house full of people to help! But Jane is a very independent woman with a tremendous determination to raise her child well. As I got to know Jane better, I would tease her that she "was a tough nut to crack."

So Mary started coming to my house every morning, at 7:30 a.m. We soon began to have our own little "routine." Her home was laid out very much like mine, so it made the transition easier. Mary would sit at my kitchen table until her bus arrived at 8:15 a.m. During those forty-five minutes, I would give her medication and breakfast. Mary loved music and could follow along with whatever song was on the radio. She must have been a savant in her ability with music. She knew all the lyrics to any song that was played, and she could not be fooled, no matter how hard you tried to stump her. To play with her, I would put on the oldies station that her mom had played in the car when they arrived in the morning. I would then try to "change the words" as I sang a song. Mary would let me get away with a mistake the first time but always corrected me by singing the proper words in a louder voice the second time around. The thought of those times makes me laugh. I can still hear her melodious voice singing, "God Bless America."

Although I only had Mary for forty-five minutes, five days a week, she became my "fifth child." She learned to know not only my home but also my family members. She would repeat their names when they entered the room and said good morning to her.

God knew that Mary would be much loved in my home, and that is why he sent her to us. Her mom, Jane, had a lot of bitterness and sadness in her life. Her husband died seven years before and left her with a broken heart. Like Gerard, when Mary was under the weather, she would throw a tantrum and try to scratch and bite. Jane was very nervous about leaving Mary with me on those mornings when Mary was acting out on the way to my home. As soon as Jane reached work, she would call to ask how Mary was doing. Even when Mary was agitated and acting out, I never told Jane. Living with autism, I knew how painful it was to hear that your child has escalated in a tantrum to hurting someone. It would not have changed anything to tell this woman, who could not do anything about it at work, that her daughter was behaving badly. Instead, I would stretch the truth and tell Jane that Mary was fine and much calmer. In my heart, I knew that those outbursts occurred at specific times of the month. When Mary had her menstrual cycle or there was a full moon, Mary would become more hyperactive and more easily agitated. Thanks to prayer, I found the patience to handle Mary better and better.

As time went on, Jane began to relax more and lowered the barriers that she had raised from all her past pain and hurt. I would joke with her about "the cement wall" around her, and I told her that it was my job to "chip away" at that wall piece by piece. We all build these emotional walls in our lives. The problem with these walls is that we often get much too comfortable behind them. Nobody wants to feel the pain that causes us to construct these walls in the first place.

If you are in need of "wall removal," I have just the man for the job. He does not charge one cent, and when he does a job, it is done the proper way so that you never have to call anyone else. When he removes the wall, he cleans up the debris and garbage that have weighed you down and prevented you from healing and growing stronger. After he finishes, you have the fragrance of a healthy soul. You know that you have become healthy because you are filled with tremendous joy, no matter what storm comes. Just call for G-O-D!

Jane and Mary were the angels that God sent to teach me about humility and love for others who are not directly related to us. This family needed help, and God chose my family to be the one that lent the helping hand. Three years passed, and my family grew to love Jane and Mary. Mary became just a part of the crazy morning routine of our home. She could hear all the goings-on: me yelling for Joseph to come down and eat breakfast; Eddie looking for something; Chrissy always late and running; and Gerard having his own autistic conversations. Even in these crazy moments, there was always an underlying joy. Some people thought I was crazy watching Mary in the mornings with all the other things I had on my plate. If only people knew how selfish my motive was for watching Mary.

When I was eighteen, I sat on my sister's porch with a couple of friends. They were talking about whether there really was a heaven, a hell, and purgatory. As a devout Catholic, I had a definite opinion on this subject. But at eighteen, I was too young to go into details with them, but I told them what I thought. I said I did not want to even *imagine* hell, let alone be there for all eternity! I also told them that I would not be "a happy camper" in purgatory either. Purgatory is where people atoned for or repented the sins they committed during life. The good thing about purgatory is that these souls are holy and have not been condemned to hell. All the souls in purgatory will eventually end up in heaven. As an adult, I now realize that the most painful part of purgatory is that you meet God face-to-face at death, and you are then separated from him to repent for all your offenses. To me, there is no greater punishment than seeing the loving face of God and then having to separate from him.

I had just finished reading a copy of *Pilgrimage to Purgatory* that I had accidentally found when I was home on a weekend visit. At eighteen, this very small book made a big impression on me. The Catholic tradition teaches that suffering, when offered to God, becomes redemptive. In other words, anything offered to God through suffering is like adding money to a "spiritual bank" to be used at a later time. Only this "bank" is in heaven, and it will pave the way to paradise when you die. On that porch, I proclaimed to my friends, and God, that I wanted to do my purgatory and repentance here on earth so that I might be able to enter heaven directly when I die. I believe God listens to eighteen-year-olds. My adult life has not been a bowl of cherries, but despite all the pain and difficulties, I have joy in knowing that I am not alone and that all I suffer is not in vain. My "bank account" in heaven is healthy, just as I hoped it would be. All my acts of love and kindness increase my account, and my suffering, anxieties, misfortunes, and disappointments are offered to God as an act of love. I am only in my forties, but I have already had such a wonderful life, and I thank God for it every day!

As much as I was helping Jane and Mary, they were helping me. The more I do for others, the more is given to me in the way of blessings from God. When I learned that Gerard was autistic, I asked God to cure Gerard if it is in his will to do so before I die. I have never given up hope that this might happen one day. I *long* for a full conversation with my son; it would be music to my ears to hear Gerard tell me all the things he has felt or wanted or needed. But even though I have never had a "conversation" with Gerard, I have always worked hard to make sure his needs are understood and met. He communicates his needs by labeling things, and his emotional needs are met through profound love. I know that he loves me and also has a deep trust in me. I tell people that Gerard's love is "not of this world." At night, before he falls asleep, I lay in bed with him, and he makes this cooing sound as he hugs and holds me. He will say the same thing each night to me, "Mama, love you," which is his way of saying that he wants me to give him lots of hugs and kisses. No matter what the day has brought, the day ends with Mama's hugs and kisses.

CHAPTER 21

A Prophecy

Because Gerard is such a fan of that famous mouse who resides in Florida, I decided to take Eddie and Gerard into the city to see the musical *Beauty and the Beast*. Gerard's teacher told me that I was brave to even attempt this. My husband, Ed, was willing to take the day off, so we made our plans. Gerard is fascinated by trains, so I thought it would be fun to travel into New York City by railroad. My mother lives only a few blocks from the railroad station, so we were able to leave the car at her house and wait for the train.

Like an idiot, I listened to everyone else and arrived at the station half an hour before the train's arrival. That half hour felt more like *ten hours* with Gerard! Talk about feeling anxious: Gerard was wringing his hands a mile a minute, repeating a million times, "Train, go to show." My husband was not helping the situation, because all he kept saying was, "I thought this was a bad idea." Little Eddie was looking at me for a response, and I was not about to show him anything but reassurance in my eyes.

Thank God the train arrived on time; otherwise, I think Gerard would have jumped onto the tracks to look for it! The actual train ride was great, and Gerard would have been very happy to stay on the train for days. He loved the motion and the lights.

When we arrived in the city, I realized that the show did not start for another hour. If we took a cab to the theater, we would have too much time to wait around. So we decided to walk from Penn

Station to the theater on Broadway. Luckily, it was a beautiful day and perfect for taking a stroll. Gerard is also obsessed with New York City and has posters and lots of New York City postcards that my cousin Fran sends him. He was taking in the whole city as we slowly made our way to the theater.

We arrived fifteen minutes before the opening of the doors. To someone unaccustomed to autism, fifteen minutes can be made to feel like a lifetime! In front of the theater, Gerard started to wring his hands and get upset that we were not going straight to our seats. When they finally let us in, we had to stand in a different hallway for another half hour. People were starting to stare at Gerard because he was getting more and more upset with each passing minute. Some people never understand autism, and I have stopped trying to explain what I need to do for my child. It is during times like these that I want to scream with helplessness. All I could do was pray and ask for help from heaven.

Within a minute of finishing my prayer, one of the ushers saw Gerard's distress. He asked if anything was wrong. I explained that Gerard was autistic and that he did not understand that we had to wait in two hallways before seeing the show. The usher could see that Gerard was upset and told us to follow him. The usher explained that normally they never seat anyone before they open the theater for the show, but they made an exception for our family. Gerard was fine once we were sitting in the theater. There, in this lovely auditorium, was Ed, Eddie, Gerard, and I, completely alone. The only other people around were the staff. We thanked the usher profusely; he was a young man in his early twenties, who had the compassion and wisdom of someone much older.

Gerard loved the show and laughed appropriately when things were funny. He enjoyed himself too much, if that is possible! I had purchased orchestra seats, so we had a wonderful view of the stage. We all enjoyed the show as much as Gerard. When the show was over, we took the boys to a nice restaurant for dinner.

Upon sitting down to eat, I should have predicted what was coming. Gerard had been very quietly saying, "No nanny's house. No train." Apparently, Gerard wanted to see all the other productions on

Broadway right then and there! We spent our entire meal trying to explain to Gerard that we would visit New York City another time and see a show. Who was I trying to kid with this line?

I had thought that if we walked back to Penn Station after dinner, we could take our time and see more of the city. But in a low, steady voice, Gerard kept repeating over and over, "No nanny's house. No train." As we got closer to Penn Station, Gerard got louder and louder. To maintain calm, I kept reassuring Gerard that everything was okay while trying to enjoy the walk with Ed and Eddie.

The only phrase that accurately describes what we faced when we reached Penn Station was "the shit hit the fan." I thought I could "outsmart" Gerard by walking around to the back entrance of Penn Station instead of through the front. But it would have made no difference even if I could have flown us through the *roof!* Gerard went into the worst tantrum I have ever experienced with him. It was now a weekday rush hour outside of Penn Station, and Gerard was lying on the cement going absolutely crazy! His screams could be heard at quite a distance. Even the homeless people stopped to take a look. Most people viewing us probably thought that we were abducting Gerard or killing him. I felt most sorry, however, for Eddie. He had seen some pretty bad tantrums in the past, but this was the worst. The only tantrum that came even close was the one at the tower ride in Florida.

Meanwhile, my husband, Ed, was getting very nervous and began pacing away from the situation and started mumbling to himself. He could not help it. All he could say was, "Liz, we are never getting out of this city. We should never have tried to take him here." The more Ed kept repeating this, the more upset Eddie became. Gerard was now lying on the filthy cement, smashing his head with his hands, and screaming at the top of his lungs. I knew that if I lost my sense of control, it was over.

So with my fear flying off the charts, I started to look around for help. Eddie got my attention by looking straight into my eyes and telling me that we needed a *miracle*. The second he said those words, I knew he was absolutely right. Nothing was going to get us out of the city but God. With all my inner strength and faith, I did not plead for help—I *claimed* it.

I was forty-one at the time but still needed the comforting advice of my mother. Even though she was miles away, I knew she could give me peace and hope. I called her on the cell phone. She immediately heard Gerard wailing in the background and told me not to try to put him on a train. She suggested that we get a taxi to take us to her house, and she would have the money ready to pay the cab driver. Mom was eighty-two at the time and gave me great directions: she was inspired by Mother Mary to guide me to where I needed to go.

I immediately tried to flag down a cab. Gerard was so out of control that I feared that someone was going to call the police and they would have to restrain him to get him into an ambulance. There was *no way* that I was going to let Eddie see that! Out of nowhere came a young man with a clipboard. He came over and told me that taxis could not stop on this street for me. He pointed to another corner of the street and said there would be a cab waiting to take us to Long Island. With Gerard completely crazed, I did not realize until later the details of the man's conversation. None of us had told him we needed a cab to take us to Long Island. Eddie could not figure out where the man and his clipboard came from.

We were able to get Gerard to the corner and get on a short line for a cab. It was strange; Gerard was trancelike on the line as if he never had that huge tantrum minutes before. I felt like I was in the *Twilight Zone.*

A cab pulled up to the curb driven by a middle-aged man. With a warm and welcoming smile, he got out of the cab and opened the back door for Eddie, Gerard, and me to sit. My husband got into the front seat. Before I could tell the driver where I needed to go or about Gerard's autism, the driver told me that he would take us to Long Island. This detail did not sink in until much later when I got home and thought about how the day had unfolded.

I gave him Mom's address and asked if he could possibly tell me how much it would cost. All he kept saying was "not to worry about the money," and told me to "relax." Anxious about how much the ride might cost, I asked politely if he could call the dispatcher to find out the fare. He did as I asked and was told the fare would be eighty dollars. Mom said she had one hundred dollars at home, and I knew I had enough on me for the tip.

I began to tell the driver about Gerard and our trip into the city and then told him about Gerard's tantrum. I then closed my eyes, waiting for the driver to tell me that if Gerard acts out in the cab, the cab would have to a stop. Instead I heard his calm voice telling me not to worry about anything. He told me that he was a minister and that we were truly blessed to have this child.

That was the last audible word I heard come from this man's mouth. It was as if switch had been turned on in the tantrum center of Gerard's brain. Within seconds, Gerard was in a carbon copy of the tantrum that he displayed outside Penn Station. I closed the Plexiglas window divider in the cab, hoping to lessen the volume of Gerard's screaming. Each time I closed the divider, the driver opened it with a beautiful smile, trying to reassure me that all was well. Because it was rush hour, we were stuck in traffic for the whole ride. I had to close the back windows because everyone was staring at our cab. I would have stared too, thinking that the people in the cab might be abducting or torturing a child.

Eddie and I tried every conceivable way of calming and diverting Gerard. Gerard wanted no part of Eddie or me. All Gerard wanted was to see the show again and stay in New York City forever. It took us forty-five minutes just to get out of Manhattan! I was terrified that the cab driver would use his power to tell me and my family "to get out of the cab now!" Gerard did not stop for even a few seconds. His screams were like something out of a horror movie. The tantrum was so severe that I could not even pray. Numbness was all I felt. Gerard was thrashing in the back of the cab and smashing a clenched fist against that Plexiglas divider. Had it been real glass, Gerard would have been in the ER with a severed artery.

The Midtown Tunnel was jammed with traffic so every car near us got quite a show. When the people in the cars passed and realized that something was wrong with Gerard, you could see their faces change from confusion to sadness for us. Gerard had hit himself so much in the head that I thought he would collapse in the cab from a brain hemorrhage. Each time he went to hit himself, I tried to hold his hand back. Then he would pinch, slap, and try to bite me.

At one point, Gerard went beyond anything I had ever witnessed in him; he gave me a blow to my face that almost turned my head around in a circle! Instead of getting angry, I was so bewildered that I burst into tears and screamed for God in the cab. I remember screaming, "Jesus, where are you, and why have you abandoned me!" As I looked up through tearful eyes, the driver was looking at me through the rearview mirror and started talking to me despite Gerard's screaming. I could not hear a word he said.

It was very strange then how things unfolded after I screamed for divine intervention. My cell phone rang, and it was my sister Ann, who is my spiritual mentor. She could hear Gerard wailing in the background. I heard her say that she knew I could not pray, and that Mom and Aunt Irene, along with Ann's family, my sister Ellen and her husband were all storming heaven with prayers for us to get home safely.

After a long and painful two-hour drive, we finally reached Mom's house. Gerard stopped throwing a tantrum as soon as we pulled up to the house. It was as if we had pulled out a plug or shut off a switch. If I had opened the back door of the cab too fast, I think I would have fallen out onto the pavement! Tired cannot even begin to describe what we felt. Eddie was so overwhelmed that I made him put my blazer over his ears in the cab. He was so exhausted that he fell asleep about five miles from Mom's house.

Before I got out of the cab, I wrote down the name of the driver and his identification number. If there was ever an unsung hero, it was this man. I was not going to stop praising him until he received the keys to the city from the mayor of New York! There simply was not enough money in the world that I could have given him for what he did for my family.

My husband took the boys into the house while I got money from my mom. As I walked back to the taxi, the man was standing outside his car door. When I went to hand him the money, he smiled and said that he could not take one dime from me. I laughed and figured he was kidding. With all that he had just gone through, he deserved *$1,000!*

He then surprised me by saying he was "honored to have driven" my son and family home. He said that he had "the gift of prophecy from the Holy Spirit," and when he saw Gerard give me that punch in the face, he knew that I was "a woman of great faith." He prophesized, "Because of that faith, you will see your son healed one day of this illness." He then told me, "God is putting you through great trials and tribulations to purify you." His key message, which he repeated several times, was that I was "on the right track and should not come off it." He told me to "Stay the course, no matter how bad the storm gets. Just keep putting your trust in God."

I put the money for the fare in his front pocket and told him that if he could not take it, then he could give it to the poor. I also wrote down my name, address, and phone number so that he could come to my home for a barbeque and a swim in the pool. I told him that I would prepare a banquet for him that would be fit for a king. He then embraced me so hard that I felt like I was getting a chiropractic adjustment! He kissed me on the cheek and told me he had to go. I laughed with him and told him that I hoped to see him again. He reassured me that we would meet again. When I tried to give him directions on how to return to the parkway, he laughed and told me he did not need directions. He said "the Holy Spirit" would bring him home.

As he drove away, I was filled with tremendous peace even though the day had been one of the hardest of my life. When I went inside the house, my sister Ellen and her husband, John, came over to see how we were. I revealed to them what this man had told me, and they were in filled with wonder. The next day, when I told my neighbors, Katie, Joan, and Anthony, the story, Anthony looked at me and said, "Liz, you know that it was an angel who drove you home, don't you? I'll put money on it that there is no one with that name who drove a cab that day to Long Island." That thought had not crossed my mind! But when I remembered how this man looked at me in the rearview mirror, it was as if he were looking *through* me.

Anthony had gotten me curious, so I decided to call all the cab companies in New York City. I ran down the list in the phonebook and gave each company the taxi driver's name. No one had an employee with that name. When I called Penn Station, they gave me the name of the taxi company that has a booth on their corner. When I told the taxi switchboard operator my story, she tried everything in her power to find this man. She explained that, by law, the driver had to have a picture ID located near the window divider facing the backseat. I told her I had seen the man's name and photo there.

I then tried calling information (411) to see if I could obtain a listing of this man in Manhattan or the other four boroughs. Nothing. I tried Nassau County, Suffolk County, Connecticut, New Jersey, Westchester County, and even as far as Pennsylvania and Maryland! After explaining the importance of finding this man, the female information operator, who was very kind, replied, "Honey, you won't find that man until you meet him in heaven. You were driven home by an angel of God."

Anthony, Joan, and Katie were not a bit surprised when I told them the outcome of my search. They laughed and joked with me, saying, "Did you expect anything else?" To this wonderful, compassionate, and truly good man, as Gerard's mother, I offer you the sincerest debt of *gratitude*. I am sorry that I did not get the chance to make you the banquet that I was planning. I guess I will have to whip something up for you when I see you in heaven!

What I took from this miraculous visit with an angel was that Gerard may be cured someday. If I had not had God and Mother Mary supporting me that day, I truly believe I would have become depressed and thought of suicide. Autism has a way of consuming even the most optimistic souls. Instead of despair and depression over Gerard's fiercest tantrum, God gave me hope that day—hope that, one day, my child will be free from this disease. My heart was filled with such joy that night going to bed, and I lay daydreaming about the day when Gerard would be completely well. Even if this does not occur during my lifetime, I live each day in hope that a cure is found—not only for Gerard but for every child under the umbrella of autism.

This experience has changed my life forever. From that day on, when Gerard acts out, I remind myself of what I was told that day. This gives me a new insight to life, and I pray each day that I am alive to witness that miracle. I pray that all children afflicted with physical or mental handicaps be made well, and that their caretakers are showered with graces and blessings to sustain them their entire lives.

The most important guidance I received that day was "to stay on track": the driver/angel prepared me for more trials and difficulties ahead. With these trials, God tests us to see if we are going to go the distance or turn back. If we turn back, then we will have to repeat the trial over and over until we have gotten it right. Many times in the past, I have come close to crossing the finish line, but my desire to control my life and my fears has caused me to bail out before the end of the race. I wind up running the same race over and over, becoming both physically and mentally exhausted. "Staying on track" to the end of the race means completely *trusting* in God. Let him do the worrying and surrender your fears to his will. If you do so, you will see things in a different light; it is our fear that blocks us from trusting God. We have free will so that we can *choose* to let God help carry our burdens.

CHAPTER 22

The Way of the Cross

We often forget in the midst of our own troubles that others are suffering too. This chapter is about our neighbors Joan and Anthony. At thirty-four years old, Anthony seemed to be in great physical health. He was a New York City fireman for two years, and his job *was* his identity because he was passionate about it. As a young boy, he had always wanted to be a fireman and was thrilled when he finally became one. Although his wife, Joan, was anxious about his safety on the job, I do not think Anthony ever gave it a thought. He was filled with energy and love, a perfect combination for any fireman. If someone needed help, Anthony was going to make sure they got it—no matter what the risk.

One winter day, I got a call from Joan telling me that Anthony was in the ER with a blood clot in his jugular vein. I had never heard of such a thing. She told me that he had a large amount of swelling at the side of his neck, and he thought it was a muscle pull. She also told me that Anthony had lost quite a bit of weight over a short period of time. As she told me his symptoms over the phone, I began getting sick to my stomach. In my heart, I already knew that Anthony had cancer. Not wanting Jane to hear the fear in my voice, I tried to reassure her and said that I would call the ER to speak to my friends about Anthony.

Before calling the hospital, I cried for ten minutes straight. This could not be possible! Such a healthy, vibrant man as Anthony had enough life in him for ten men! When I finally called the hospital, they told me that Anthony was not being a "cooperative patient." Because of the blood clot, he was ordered to strict bed rest. "Good luck!" I said, laughing, "He'll never use a bedpan or urinal, and if you leave him long enough in the ER, he will probably take the place of one of the physicians!" There was no news yet on his tests, and he was being transferred to a room later that day. Calling Joan back, I could hear the anxiety in her voice. All I could do for them was to pray.

It was later revealed that Anthony had prostate cancer—which is very rare in young men. Because of his age and youthful hormones, the cancer was able to spread much faster than in elderly men. For months, they could not pinpoint an origin for his cancer, so he had to take several chemotherapies along with multiple radiation therapies, which left him very sick. When I visited him, after he got home from the hospital, he consoled *me* as I broke into tears just looking at him. He was full of hope that the chemotherapy would destroy the cancer.

If I were to remember a time in my life that I prayed the hardest, it would have to be at this time. One day, deep in prayer for Anthony, I begged God to send me a sign that Anthony would be well. It was a cold winter's day, and the first thought to enter my mind was *watermelons!* I became upset with God; how could I possibly see any watermelons in the middle of winter? But God sends signs of confirmation in many different ways, and it is our faith in knowing that they come from God that makes the absurd become true. The watermelons were a sign just like my butterflies.

When I called Joan to tell her about the sign the Lord had given me to comfort me about Anthony, Joan could not believe what I was telling her. Minutes before, the firemen from Anthony's firehouse had delivered cold cuts and rolls for lunch to celebrate Anthony's return from the hospital. They did not know what to bring Joan, so they gave her a container of *watermelon!* After that, just like my butterflies, numerous pictures and objects with watermelons kept appearing. It was not the watermelon itself that mattered; it was the *faith* behind the sign showing that *God is here.*

A month after Anthony became ill, Joan told us that she was expecting another baby. This would be her fifth child. Joan was so brave in facing the terrible disease of her husband and being pregnant at the same time. This was truly a heavy cross to bear. Now she had to take care of her sickly husband, her other children, and her own growing body. She suffered from morning sickness for the first few months, which only added to her troubles. But Joan and Anthony were blessed with a wonderfully supportive family and devoted friends. Anthony's firemen buddies could not do enough for both of them. They came out on their days off to work on the house and complete anything that needed to be done. They loved Anthony as their brother. It is the same love that God wants us to show all of our brothers and sisters everywhere. If each of us could be this supportive of everyone, there would be no wars and no hate.

Anthony's illness allowed me to spend a lot of time with him. He would go past my home on his daily walk, and we would talk about many things. Anthony and Joan were very receptive to my religious beliefs, so I could always tell them openly that I was praying hard for all of them. Likewise, Joan's mother, Rita, became my "fence friend." For diversion, Rita would walk the kids up and down the block, and we would talk over my fence in the front yard. We had wonderful conversations and would laugh at the dopiest things—we needed to at this time. Even in the midst of sadness, God gives us reasons for joy, which we must always treasure and seek out.

One of the hardest things was seeing Anthony lose his hair and his weight. He had beautiful thick black hair and a very healthy and strong physique. Although our culture looks at the physical body as being most important, I was not interested in Anthony's outer surface. I was most interested in his *soul*. Whenever I visited with him, which was at least once a week, I would bring some food treat, as well as some religious article. Each time, I left him with a short story or description of God, Mother Mary, or of a particular saint. On some visits, when he was so blue and depressed, all I could do was give him a big kiss and pray like I never prayed before. He always accepted what I brought with the sincerest thanks. I would have liked to have visited Anthony more often, but I did not want to invade their privacy. Joan later told me that after I left, Anthony always wished that I would visit more often. He told her that he was always filled with hope and felt stronger after I visited. Those visits meant so much to *me* too!

It was during this time that Ed and I decided we needed to renovate our house. At first, we were not sure whether to renovate with Anthony being so sick. The renovation would involve gutting the entire house and having some plumbing and electrical work done that could not wait. We finally decided to go ahead with our plans and hire a contractor. When our blueprints came in the mail, we became excited about imagining the finished house. Of course, all our neighbors, including Anthony and Joan, came to see the drawings. It was actually good for Anthony because he was now home on permanent disability and would be able to observe the work in progress.

But there was no way we would be able to gut the entire house and *live* there at the same time with Gerard. We decided to move into my mother's home temporarily, which is about twelve miles away. The job would take about five months. The hardest part of the move was not leaving our home but leaving Anthony and Joan, Katie and Fred, and all the neighborhood kids. They were our "extended family." As it turned out, we would still see some of them briefly every day because I had to travel every morning and afternoon to drop off and pick up the kids at the bus stop. Jane worried that it would be too much for me to pick up Mary two hours earlier every morning for her bus. Jane kept telling me that it was too much for me and that it would not work. But when God wants something done, he gives you all you need to complete the task.

Each morning, I would be up at 5:00 a.m. to pack lunches and iron clothes. The kids would shower the night before. By 6:40 a.m., I would have Eddie, Gerard, and Joseph in the car heading to Jane's house, and we would arrive around 7:00 a.m. so that Jane could leave for work. The school buses did not arrive for over an hour, so we had to wait. That winter, the weather was quite bad. Mom kept telling me that I was doing too much running back and forth each day, but I knew what needed to be done. Jane was so thankful that I traveled daily for Mary, and, in retrospect, I am very glad I did as things would turn out later. I would have traveled *a hundred miles or more* for Mary. I did not want Jane to look for a new sitter, and I knew how comfortable Mary was with my family. Plus, I was asking for a really big favor from God. This was the least I could do to ask for God's help with Anthony. Every time I called Joan to ask about Anthony, she would always tell me that Anthony wanted to know when we were coming home. For some reason, I think Anthony feared that we might forget him. That was *not* possible. I was praying even harder for their entire family.

We moved to my mother's home at the end of 2000. God gave me many blessings while we lived with my mom. Those blessings would sustain me through the rough months ahead. They allowed me to face some very trying and sad times with a sense of hope and joy, instead of despair and depression.

We returned to our newly renovated house in June 2001. By this time, Anthony had full metastasis of the cancer to his bones. He was painfully thin and was in a tremendous amount of pain. The bones of his legs, shoulder, spinal column, and skull were all affected. Because he could not tolerate morphine, they put him on a methadone drip to control the pain. On one occasion, his pain became so unbearable that he told me that he screamed for hours in a pain that could not be described. He then told me something that will stay with me for the rest of my life: Anthony said that the pain was so excruciating that he felt like he was *being nailed to the cross*. He cried so hard during his description of this event and looked into my eyes for a response. He probably did not expect what I said next. I told him he was "*lucky* to have shared in the ultimate sacrifice of God." Anthony had felt what Jesus experienced in his death and passion during the Crucifixion. On this visit, I told Anthony that Anthony the Man had no use for all this pain and suffering; but if he offered it with love to God, the pain, suffering, and turmoil would turn into graces. I told Anthony to offer his daily suffering each morning to God in the name of Jesus, through the intercession of Mother Mary, and for the glorification of the Father. This period is very difficult for me to write about, and I have to stop often in order to compose myself and tell you about these events.

On his thirty-sixth birthday, Anthony thanked me for everything I had ever done for him. Before me, I saw a man that I no longer recognized from his outward appearance. He was confined to a wheelchair or couch for sitting and the bed for resting. He was unable to walk on his own. Despite his sickly aspect, Anthony never lost the will to live in hope. That was all God had expected from him. Anthony told me privately that night that if he ever lost control of his bladder or his bowels, then he wanted to die. He thought this would be too much for him to bear.

In August 2001, Katie and I went over at night to help turn and position Anthony for Joan. He had developed a bedsore on his lower spine, and we changed the dressing whenever it was needed. When I entered the bedroom, I could see that his breathing had changed, and I did not want to believe it. How could this be? I had received many watermelon signs telling me that he would be okay. I suddenly needed to cry, so I made an excuse that I was going to make him some ice chips in my kitchen. After a much-needed cry, I made the ice chips and came back.

When I kissed Anthony good night, he motioned for me to come closer to him. He had something to tell me. I thought he was about to leave me some profound words of wisdom, and I almost stopped to ask him if I should get a pen and paper to write it down. As I listened intently, he asked me if Joan had put the air conditioner on "*fan mode* instead of *air control*"? He went on to tell me that he had been sweating all day, and Joan did not seem to know what she was doing with the air conditioner! He thought that I knew how to fix the situation. I looked at him and said, "Are you kidding? Is that what you wanted to tell me?" This is the kind of humor that God likes to send me. Even in the midst of sorrow, there was something we could laugh about! I corrected the air-conditioning. Joan had put it on fan mode at a higher temperature because she did not want Anthony to get a chill.

Early the next morning, Katie and I went to see Anthony. His breathing was labored, and he was unresponsive. There was only

Katie, Joan, and me with him. I did not want Anthony to leave us, and I was perplexed by the signs of watermelons, which had given me such strength during this time. In this state of uneasiness, I felt totally confused. God was not yet ready to reveal to me the watermelon's true meaning.

As Joan talked to Katie, I stood right near where Anthony lay. When I put my hand down on the bed, it was warm and wet. I looked down and saw that Anthony was incontinent with urine, something he told me he could not handle. As soon as I saw that, it was time for me to let go and alter my prayers into a different direction. I whispered in his ear that it was time for him to go *home*. He had earned enough graces to give him an upper room in heaven with a view. God would not let Anthony's suffering, pain, sorrow, and depression go to waste; Anthony could redeem them in for a trip to everlasting paradise.

Before the rest of the family and friends arrived, Katie and I had the privilege of bathing Anthony. There is something very spiritual in bathing someone who is dying. It is done with a level of dignity and respect that cannot be described. It was also a very tender way of showing my profound love for my friend. Before anyone arrived, I was able to give Anthony the biggest hug and lots of what the kids on my block refer to as "Aunt Lizzie Kisses."

All of Anthony and Joan's family, along with their closest friends, were present when the priest anointed him and gave him last rites. Anthony had been on an oxygen mask for quite some time. Suddenly, Anthony went from an unresponsive state to being able to pull himself up in the bed, pull off his oxygen mask, and started to reach forward. I asked him if he were in pain. His answer was a definitive *no*. He looked right through the crowd that held a vigil around his bed. He kept stretching out his arms and reaching until he reached what he was looking for. He then sat back and went *home*.

What I had witnessed was his transference from this world into heaven. Even though I could hear the family members sobbing, I felt this tremendously warm feeling of the Holy Spirit, letting me know that Anthony had gone where many people want to go. It filled me with profound joy. I looked down at his chest and saw his green scapular (a religious cloth), and behind him, on the headboard, were all the religious articles I had given him over the past nineteen months. Within a few minutes of Anthony's passing, it became clear to me what the watermelon signs had meant. Anthony, for his suffering and faithfulness, would reap wonderful rewards in heaven. God's watermelons were signs that Anthony had been healed and made well—not in the eyes of the world but in divine eyes where his soul was completely restored.

The day after Anthony's death, I had to go to my cousin's bridal shower. At first, I thought I should cancel my plans, but then I thought of the life that Anthony had lived. His life was full of life and laughter. He had completed his journey and was now reaping his reward.

In all my sadness, I had forgotten to buy a shower gift. I had planned on getting a gift certificate, so I went to pick one up. Thinking about what had transpired the day before, I felt like I was in a fog at the store. I thought of Joan and her children and what would be expected of them in the next few days toward the funeral. As I proceeded to the cashier to buy a gift certificate, a young man came up to me and asked if I needed help. I explained to him that I only needed a gift certificate and, for some reason, apologized for my fog-like appearance. Something told me to tell the young man about the loss of Anthony and my new house. The young man looked at me and told me that he had just the thing for my newly renovated house. He went over to a display counter and held up an outdoor signpost for me. The front of it was facing him, so I could not see the writing on it. I told him that I did not need anything like that, but he was kindly and insistent and said this was for my home. As he handed it to me, I turned the sign around to read its writing. There was a watering can marked with a *watermelon* on it and the words "Garden of Plenty." When I saw the watermelon, I broke into tears! Then when I looked up to thank the young man, he was gone! Through my tears, I tried to find him, but, of course, I never did. There are no coincidences. This sign confirmed in my heart that the young man was an angel sent by Anthony to let me know that all was well. This was a "welcome home" gift from Anthony for my newly renovated home. This would be one of many heavenly gifts sent from my dear friend Anthony.

Anthony was given a wake and funeral fit for a dignitary. He might not have been a government leader, but he was the "mayor" of our block. Soon after Anthony died, a longtime priest and friend came from the city to bless Anthony at home. This priest also presided over Anthony's funeral mass accompanied by two other priests. During the priest's homily, he told us what Anthony had said during his several hospitalizations. Anthony believed that he was "carrying a cross." He did not know the purpose for this cross, other than that he offered it each day to God. Anthony thought he might be carrying it so that one of the children who suffered from cancer at that hospital could be made well. The priest was also very impressed that Anthony wore the green scapular and had a shelf behind his bed with pictures of Mary and the saints. The priest then spoke about heaven, which he described as the most beautiful garden where Anthony was now free of pain, stress, and all the ills of life. The priest said the word *garden* so many times that Katie whispered in my ear, "That's where your front sign slogan came from: Garden of Plenty!" As much as I wanted to cry, I could not. My soul felt like it was going to burst with happiness for my friend. He was truly home in the presence of God, Mary, and all the saints and angels of heaven.

Driving from the church to the cemetery was a twenty-minute ride, and Anthony had a fireman's funeral, which was fit for a king. There were police escorts on motorcycles at the front of the procession. At one point, a driver, who was pulling out of a driveway, did not see the motorcycle officer and accidentally knocked him off the bike. The entire funeral procession came to a halt. People got out of their cars and ran toward the injured policeman. Thank God, the policeman was not seriously hurt, but he did need medical attention. As the traffic on the other side of the street came to a halt, I looked up at a truck directly opposite the procession. It was a large tractor trailer painted with a logo covered by *watermelons.* I have seen banana logos before, but I have never seen so many watermelons on a truck in my life! When my husband and Katie saw it, they could not believe it either. We knew it was a sign for Anthony.

After Anthony was buried, Rita, Anthony's mother-in-law, came up to me during the post-funeral meal at the restaurant. She asked me if I saw "the truck." I laughed, and I told her that I think *everyone* saw that truck. You could not miss it if you tried. These watermelons were gifts from heaven, telling me that Anthony was not gone. Instead, his life had undergone a change. His story and his photo in my home are a constant reminder of a brave soul who stayed on the track and received his reward in paradise.

Now our concerns turned to Joan, who is a most faithful and obedient daughter to God and was the most faithful, loving, and obedient wife to Anthony. Joan and Anthony had been very much in love. Imagine the shock and pain of expecting your fifth child when your husband has terminal cancer! Joan was forty at the time, and between taking care of herself and their four children, she was already tired. Add to that the stress that your beloved has a fatal illness—this left Joan completely exhausted. Anthony had wanted to die at home, and Joan never left his side for a moment. She would stay in the hospital during his hospitalizations even though the only place for her to sleep was in a chair by his bed. Their ordeal went on for nineteen months. There were times when she would pull up in the car looking like she was in a daze or sleeping. I would then pray and ask her guardian angel to always get her safely where she needed to go.

Joan's tremendous love and devotion to Anthony never faltered even as he became more ill. She dug down deeper to find the strength that she needed to carry this very heavy cross. When Anthony went to heaven, he left her the *pain* of his loss. It has been two years since his death, and missing him is still very painful. My prayer for her is that one day she will realize that Anthony loved her so much that he wanted her to carry a heavy cross to earn graces quickly so that she can join him in heaven when her time comes.

You may wonder why I include stories about people other than Gerard in this book. The reason I write about these people is that they have all added to the blessings I have received since Gerard was diagnosed with autism. Anthony was always very kind to Gerard and everyone he knew—and God so loved Anthony that he chose him to share in his suffering at the Crucifixion. Stories like Anthony's confirm for me the complete joy to be found in the midst of carrying a heavy cross. Accepting God's will is not easy, but despite the many difficulties, the outcome brings true joy and contentment. It opens your eyes to see the world in the way God intended.

CHAPTER 23

More Sadness and a Challenge

Although you try to prepare yourself for someone's passing, it still hurts so much when they do. Anthony will never be forgotten by anyone who knew him. Now that Anthony is in heaven, we are lucky to have him as a wonderful intercessor for us all.

Another sad trial soon followed. A couple of days before Anthony's death, my next-door neighbor Frank became ill. Frank and Lorraine never had children of their own and were in their late seventies. Lorraine did not drive, and her family lived out of state, so she needed our help because Frank had episodes of dizziness. When I went to check on them and saw Frank, I knew he needed to be admitted to a hospital for dehydration. He had lost twenty-five pounds in a month. Frank was then diagnosed with colon cancer, which had already metastasized to his other organs. God did not give me time to be blue or melancholy about Anthony's death. I was much too busy driving Lorraine back and forth to the hospital two times a day. Once Frank was admitted to the hospital, he went downhill rapidly and died two weeks later.

Lorraine was married to Frank for fifty-years and loved him more than anything. They were each other's life. God blessed Frank even as he lay dying: Frank was not aware of his illness prior to his final two-week period, and he never suffered any pain even though the cancer had spread to the bones of his spine. God knew that Lorraine could not have handled a long illness with Frank, so in his mercy, he spared her this. Today, Lorraine has been blessed by her own growing independence. She is doing things that she never thought possible. God has closed one door for her but opened another.

Between these major events, Gerard continued to have the outbursts or agitated states that often occur with autism. Despite their severity, I was now armed with enough trust in God that the tantrums stopped affecting me the way that they had in the past. I had given these episodes too much power. I had let them fuel my fear. Once I removed the fear, I was better able to deal with the actual tantrum instead of beating myself up about them.

In the summer of 2001, Chrissy was nineteen and a young adult. She took a job as a camp counselor and loved it. She began to think that she would like to work with children in the future, so she decided to become a teacher's aide for the school year. The school was a camp during the summer months and also a nursery to K-level school during the rest of the year. Chrissy had been dating a boy for about a year and a half; and toward the end of their relationship, they would fight, make up, and then fight again. They finally broke up, and about two months later, I noticed Chrissy was ill for over a week with what I assumed was an intestinal virus.

One day, a day that is written in my internal scrapbook forever in permanent markers, Chrissy came home during lunch and told me that she was very sick to her stomach. As a "dopey mother," I recommended dry crackers and some ginger ale. I even suggested that she call the doctor since this "virus" had lasted over a week! I am not sure if I got the complete sentence out of my mouth, before she started crying and telling me that she was *pregnant*. I know I heard her but thought that maybe I was dreaming.

Instead of reacting to the situation at hand, I told her to "hold that thought." Then I went into the family room to hyperventilate by myself. As I walked further into the room, I saw my picture of the Blessed Mother. This is one of my favorite pictures of Mother Mary, and it is called the "Madonna of the Streets." Mother Mary is holding the infant Jesus in her arms with such love and compassion.

I prayed and asked Mother Mary to let me respond the way that she wanted me to when I returned to Chrissy. I was then struck with the knowledge that I was going to *stand by Chrissy for the rest of her life*!

I slapped myself on the cheek and said, "Get over it, Liz! She didn't tell you that she was dying or that she killed someone!" As I got to the kitchen, Chrissy was bent over in her chair, sobbing. All my worries were replaced by what Mother Mary wanted me to do for my child. I ran over to Chrissy and held her on my lap for over half an hour. We both cried. The only thing I said was that I loved Chrissy more than anything and that I was so proud that she loved me enough to come and tell me what was troubling her.

My pride in my daughter went beyond the point of her being able to come to me right away. I believe that the inclusion of God and Mary in our lives has led to this openness and trust that our children feel for us as parents. Chrissy and Eddie always tell me everything. Sometimes, they tell me too much information! There are times when I hope that they will forget the ending of a particular story or event—but they never do!

As a mother, I have always given my children my views on many topics including premarital sex. My children have always known how I feel on certain issues, so it has never been a surprise to them. However, you can lead a horse to water, but you cannot make it drink.

I am open with my children about medical and moral issues. When Chrissy was eighteen, I took her for her first gynecological exam. The doctor is a friend of mine, so he was a bit embarrassed to ask me to leave when he and Chrissy were talking in his office. He was then surprised when Chrissy told him that she did not want me to leave. She said that there was nothing she could not say in front of me. He was amazed and said it was very rare that a girl her age did not keep secrets from her mother. He then laughed when I asked him if he could "teach Chrissy how to do that." I am very happy that our kids feel loved and secure enough to know that no matter what they tell us, we will always love them. We may not condone or accept all their behavior or actions, but they are always loved. Likewise Jesus and Mary love us unconditionally, even with all the problems we possess. They do not approve of all we do or say, but they remain faithful to us in their unconditional love. Chrissy knows in her heart that she is deeply loved by us and that she can always come to us.

Chrissy decided to have the baby, and I was so proud that she chose life. People laugh at me when I tell them that I was born pro-life. This issue has always been a passion of mine. In my heart and through much prayer, I have come to believe that if women and men were properly educated about abortion and how heinous a crime it is, they would not support it in any way. I then went a step further and educated myself on the factual aspects of this procedure. It horrifies me that anyone with a sincere heart or conscience can see it as a choice. I have many friends who are prochoice, and I love them for who they are, but I will never see their point of view on this issue. God's most important creation is life, and the sanctity of life should be protected at all costs. Chrissy chose the harder road by having the baby; but in the end, it is the easier one to travel because God will be there to guide her through all the turns, hills, valleys, and dangerous curves that we all encounter in life.

My family, friends, and neighbors were all very accepting of Chrissy's situation. I warned everyone that if they shunned my daughter, then they shunned me. For all the girls who have had to make this decision alone because they had no support or love behind them, my heart goes out to you. Some girls are truly abandoned by their family and friends at this time, and the pain of abandonment can be devastating.

We tend to look at events like this as "disasters" in our lives. But when you stop and take a moment to just talk with God, he shows you that these events are actually small and manageable. Because Chrissy was no longer involved with the baby's father, this journey would be harder for her. But it was also a time of true growth in both responsibility and independence. Through these events, God was molding my daughter into an even stronger independent woman.

Now that we had a new baby to contemplate, my husband was very supportive from the beginning. This would be our first grandchild, and I was already in love with him or her from the moment Chrissy told me she was pregnant. In the first few months, Chrissy had morning sickness and had to adjust to the many changes pregnancy brings. She went from constantly running around to see friends to staying at home to rest and take care of herself.

She drove me crazy with her new dietary requirements, and I wound up hiding some of those baby books and magazines. I never cooked such healthy food in my life! It was making me *sick*. Give me a big hotdog with sauerkraut and chips on the side, and I am in heaven! All the healthy food made me take antacids for chronic heartburn. With all the fruit Chrissy ate, the baby should be born with a pineapple or kiwi on its head. The minute the baby was born, I headed to the nearest burger joint for the biggest, fattest cheeseburger with a side order of fries and vanilla shake!

All kidding aside, Chrissy's decision to choose life benefited her in many ways. It began my daughter's own journey in faith. Some things cannot be taught. They have to be lived to be learned. If I am going to teach my children about God and Mother Mary's unconditional love and tolerance, then I have to step up to the plate and be faithful and obedient to God also. For me, this came in the form of Gerard's autism, where I had to learn to sacrifice to give him a life filled with love, compassion, and dignity. Now Chrissy was on a similar spiritual journey with her pregnancy.

We had now returned to our newly renovated home. Our first Christmas there was wonderful, and we threw a big party with sixty-four guests. Ed and I love to throw old-fashioned house parties where people feel warm, relaxed, and welcome. Between our families and our neighbors, we have over sixty people to invite! I am nuts about Christmas, and I love to decorate and get into the whole spirit of this beautiful season. God and Mother Mary have always blessed our parties, and I always tell people that the reason they enjoy themselves in our home is not because of the good food and drink, but because of the love of God and Mother Mary that dwells in our home. God and Mother Mary are our permanent guests who live in our home and accompany us through life.

We had so much to be thankful for: Chrissy was doing well in her new job and was feeling better. The boys had a bigger home to make a mess in, and I was busy trying to finish all the painting and trim work from the previous summer. Gerard loved the new house, which now had a nice-sized playroom on the first floor for him. This gave him his own private space. Here we kept his toys, music, books, television, VCR, and video games. Gerard was thrilled to have this playroom, and the room helped me with Gerard's autism more than I imagined.

When we had planned the renovations, I sat down with the contractor and explained how important it was for the home to be set up according to Gerard's needs. The contractor had other ideas; he wanted to put in a larger living room. We had already planned a large family room, so a small living room was more than adequate. Thank God I did not change my mind! Today, Gerard goes into his playroom and shuts the door to relax and unwind. It is a safe haven where he has had many hours of enjoyment. I frequently check on him and go to see if he wants company. If he wants company, he lets me in and loves me. If he does not want anyone else around, he politely says, "Excuse me," which is his way of saying, "Get lost."

Time flew by. Before we knew it, it was time for Chrissy's level 2 sonogram. The father of the baby was willing to take Chrissy for the sonogram, and they were gone nearly three hours. I assumed it took so long because they had to wait to talk about the results, so I did not give it much thought. When Chrissy got home, she was very upset. The radiologist said he had a hard time getting a good picture of the baby's heart because of the baby's position. I could tell Chrissy did not believe him; she knew that there was something wrong with the baby. She scheduled another level 2 sonogram with a pediatric cardiologist. Unaware of how the sonogram appeared, I could only give Chrissy moral support and pray for my grandchild. As soon as Chrissy went to bed that night, I called my mom. I told her to call my sisters and Aunt Irene and have them start praying for Chrissy and the baby.

The following week, Chrissy was scheduled for her second sonogram. I went with her this time, but all I could do was rub the top of her head and reassure her that everything was going to be all right. The pediatric cardiologist told us that the baby had a very serious heart defect called *transposition of the great arteries*. This meant that the pulmonary artery was switched with the aortic artery. In addition, the baby had a large *ventricular hole* and significant *aortic stenosis* (narrowing of the major blood vessel that supplies oxygenated blood to the entire body). The doctor told us that the situation was quite dangerous and recommended a specialist at a New York City hospital to do the necessary surgery when the baby was born. Even with surgery, there was no guarantee that the baby would survive.

As Chrissy cried, I felt extreme pain in my own heart. Here was my child feeling despair over the possible loss of her child, and all I could do was hug her and tell her to trust in God. At that point, another doctor came in and told Chrissy that it was very important that she have an amniocentesis to see if the baby had any other defects so Chrissy could decide whether she wanted to terminate her pregnancy. As the doctor said this, a sick feeling came over me. Before I even formed a response, Chrissy's assertive personality, which sometimes got her in trouble, became music to my ears. Chrissy had choice words for this doctor and started by telling him that she was not having an amniocentesis. She argued that whatever the baby was born with was in God's will and not hers. She concluded that if her baby were to die after birth, then at least she had given it the chance to live and it was in God's hands. She told the doctor not to bring up the subject again.

Standing next to Chrissy, I wanted to clap and yell, "Bravo." I suddenly realized that Chrissy *had been listening* to me all those years when I had thought she suffered from "parental deafness." She heard me the whole time, and now she was doing the preaching. Instead of leaving the hospital worried and anxious, I left knowing that God was not going to let my daughter down. I had reached a level of faith where I completely trusted God's will, and now this gift was being passed to my daughter! This spiritual legacy had been passed from my grandparents to my parents to me, and Chrissy would continue the family tradition.

After we all had a good cry for the unborn baby, we started to think only positive thoughts. Our family offered a Rosary every night for the baby's well-being and asked Jesus to take care of the baby. I prayed that Mother Mary would fill Chrissy with peace through the next four months of her pregnancy. The baby was fine while *in utero* because it was getting oxygen through fetal circulation—which bypassed the problem areas. Many wonderful people sent us prayer cards and many thoughtful gestures were given to Chrissy during this time. I kept telling Chrissy that because she chose life, she would see what God had planned for her. She was very positive and adopted the attitude that the future was not in her hands. Whatever God willed was going to be done.

I tried to return our home to normal as much as possible. But this was hard because, as a nurse, I realized the seriousness of the situation. As Chrissy's mom, however, I knew that God could make miracles happen. I had a direct connection to heaven through Anthony's intercession, and I prayed to Anthony daily for help in this matter.

Chrissy was about to turn twenty, and her birthday served as a good distraction. Every year, I let my kids choose what they would like me to make for their birthday dinner. Chrissy wanted every living creature in the ocean, so I prepared all kinds of seafood dishes. The house was decorated with flowers and balloons, and we had a lovely dinner and cake for her. I remember looking around the table and having a wonderful sense of peace. It should have been a warning to me about what lay ahead. God was giving me "the calm before the storm."

CHAPTER 24

Disaster?

Two days after Chrissy's birthday was Valentine's Day. It was a beautiful, warm, and sunny day; and I had an appointment in the morning. The errand would not take long, so I took Joseph with me, and then we went to the local shopping mall. At the mall, they have a train and carousel ride that Joseph loves to go on. We got some lunch and ice cream, and made a quick visit to the toy store. In all, we were gone about two and a half hours.

On the ride home, I was planning a special meal for Valentine's Day. It almost felt like spring, and I felt so happy with Joseph. There is no feeling as special as being in complete joy with your life. Gerard's autism had taught me that I should learn how to enjoy life whenever possible. So, even in the midst of turmoil and craziness, I try my hardest to find the delight in each situation.

When I pulled up to our house, I noticed water running down our driveway. My first response was to look up at the sky, but the sky was crystal blue without a single cloud. Then I thought that it might be snow that had melted on the roof—but there was no snow. I started to hope that Chrissy had come home from her job at lunchtime to wash her car, but that was not likely either. As I walked toward the door, I saw that the water was running in a steady stream *from my house!* When I opened the front door, water gushed toward my feet. There was over *three inches of water* on the entire first floor! My kitchen ceiling was pouring water from everywhere. The chandelier hanging over the kitchen table had water flowing from all eight of its glass globes. All I needed was a statue and a couple of pigeons, and my kids would have thought it was a fountain in Italy! Water was pouring down the front and from the insides of all my kitchen cabinets. The horrible sound of water cascading from my ceilings is a sound that I will never forget.

As I continued to walk through the house, I realized that the ceiling was already falling down in the family room from the weight of the water. The carpeting and the furniture were soaked in at least three inches of water. The living and dining room ceilings were sound, but the wood floor was ruined.

I went into shock. This could *not* be possible. We had gone through so much to renovate the house, and now all our hard work was destroyed by a flood. All I could think to do was call my neighbors Fred and Katie. I had not even hung up the phone when Fred was in my kitchen, lying on the floor in the water, shutting off the main valve. Katie could not even look me in the face, because she felt so sad. I kept repeating over and over that there had to be a reason God allowed this to happen. Katie finally had to slap me in the face and tell me that I was in shock. We laugh now when I remind her of that day. Fred began using his wet-dry vacuum to remove some of the water. In the meantime, I contacted the insurance company to let them know what happened.

My mom usually calls me several times a day, and when she heard what happened, she burst into tears. All she kept saying was, "How much more can God give you?" It was not until some time later that I figured out why God gave us this disaster. Within an hour, the insurance carrier sent over a cleanup crew to help us. My sisters Ellen and Ann and their husbands also came right over to help. They could not believe the state of the house. It was later determined that the flood was caused by a mistake of the contractor whom we hired. This contractor had subcontracted the plumbing work to a plumber who never insulated my hose bib-pipe, which ran through an area of the attic that was very dark and cold. The pipe froze during the winter, and the buildup of water flooded my entire first floor.

It took hours of everyone's hard work to get somewhat organized. The cleanup crew sent by the insurance company would come back the next morning to gut the walls because they were completely water-damaged, along with the rugs and wood floor. Ed and Chrissy went to the nearest department store to buy plastic bins for storage. We stayed up for hours drying all my dishes, glasses, silverware, pots, and pans, and packing them into these bins. It was like moving all over again.

I was so tired of packing. I had packed up the entire house to move to my mom's for the renovation of the house. After living with Mom for five months, I packed up again to move back home and then unpacked. Now I had to pack up again, the *third time* in nine months! It was not until I got into bed that night that it really hit me, and I began sobbing. The strange part was that I was not angry with God. Something in my heart told me that he would show me why this happened to us—and he eventually did.

The days that followed were even harder. First of all, it was still the dead of winter. The insurance adjuster wanted to know if we wanted to be put up in a hotel because of the condition of the house. This was not a viable option because Gerard would never tolerate another move. So I tried my best to prepare the troops for what lay ahead. When the cleanup crew came back to gut my kitchen and family room walls, they put up plastic sheeting with a zipper so that we could access the kitchen. This plastic barrier would keep the dust to a minimum in the other rooms during the reconstruction. To tear up the ruined carpeting in the family room, we had to move all our furniture from this room into the living room. The wood floor in the living and dining room was also removed, leaving us to live on a cement slab. We were left with a twelve-by-twelve-foot room on the first floor, which held all the downstairs furniture. We had large plastic bins everywhere to hold our dry food, plates, utensils, and so on. Plus, the ironing board and everything we needed to run the house were jammed into that same space. We would have to live this way for the next four months.

Gerard was so confused that he would come out of his playroom more and more often to have a tantrum in that small space. It made me appreciate how lucky we were to have all that extra space before the flood! I wondered whether I had been as thankful as I should have been for all the wonderful blessings that God had given me. The flood gave me a lot of food for thought.

The upstairs bedrooms were filled with bins of all the stuff that had to be moved out of the first floor. No matter how much I tried to clean or straighten up, it always looked like a mess. My kitchen cabinets were deemed unusable because they had significant water damage so they were all removed. We were left with a gutted shell of a kitchen and a gutted family room. It was freezing in those rooms because the insulation and wallboard were ripped out. The empty kitchen now housed only a stove and refrigerator, and I would prepare breakfast and dinner with a jacket and gloves on. During this time, I kept offering all my struggles, anxieties, and sorrows to God in return for the healing of my grandchild. We had no television downstairs, except in Gerard's playroom, so we all watched it together in Eddie's bedroom upstairs. We had a lot of family *togetherness*. We spent most of our time in the dining room on the concrete slab, which I had to sweep twenty times a day. I then started to realize that God gave us this flood in order to distract us from dwelling on the condition of Chrissy's baby. We were so busy with the house that we literally could not give our fears a second thought. We prayed daily and let God take care of the baby in the way that it was meant to be.

My insurance carrier sent a contractor to finish the reconstruction. I prayed that this man would be honest and trustworthy in God's eyes. When I opened the door, I was thrilled to see a familiar face: William, along with his partner Michael, had installed my wood floor prior to the flood. I was very happy with their work and was so glad to see them again. William knew about Gerard's autism and was very compassionate and sympathetic. He could not believe what had happened to our house and said that he was going to redo the work in the proper way. He assured us that everything would come out great—and it did. I trusted William and knew God had answered my prayers.

CHAPTER 25

Sorrow and Joy

William and his crew started to work on our house in March 2002. During that time, Jane brought her autistic daughter, Mary, to us each morning as usual. Even Mary had to go through an "adjustment" after the flood. She was used to sitting at my kitchen table in the morning while she ate her breakfast and waited for her bus. Now sitting in our crowded dining room was a new transition for her too. I do not think it really mattered where she sat as long as she could hear my kids' voices in the background and me singing the wrong words to songs on the radio to stump her. But there was no stumping Mary—if the television show *Name That Tune* were still running, Mary would have been a winner! She had a true gift for music.

When we first moved home from staying with my mom, I noticed a change in Mary. I knew she loved me, but she seemed even closer to me when we moved back. Eddie once commented that it was as if Mary knew that I had traveled back and forth, each day for five months, to take care of her because I really loved her. What I did not realize then was that God was filling my heart with wonderful memories of love to sustain me through one of the hardest and most difficult experiences of my life.

Although the flood took a lot out of my family, I reminded myself that God was kind to keep us so busy that we did not have time to think of anything else. Easter vacation was coming, and that meant the kids would be home for ten days. *Ten days* in the jam-packed dining room together; if that did not test your faith, nothing did!

It was Monday of Holy Week, and I went out to the car to get Mary as I had done for the past three years. Jane always gave me Mary's medication for the week on Monday mornings. But Jane was running late that morning and forgot to bring the medication. She was very upset about forgetting it because it was Mary's antiseizure medicine. I told Jane to give me her house key and I would go get it.

When I got Mary settled inside, I told Chrissy what I intended to do. Chrissy yelled at me that she could not be late for work and that it was not my duty to worry about Mary's medication. I tried to explain to Chrissy that, as a mother, I could never send Mary on the bus knowing that Mary could possibly have a seizure and get hurt. Besides, Mary was like one of my own children. Mary sat there without knowing what had just transpired, or so I thought.

I drove the two and a half miles as quickly as I could, without speeding, to get Mary's medicine. On the way back, I planned how I would give Mary her medication, then shower Gerard and get him dressed while Mary ate her breakfast. Each day, I mixed Mary's medication with either fruit yogurt or flavored applesauce so she would not taste its bitterness.

When I got home, I mixed it as usual and stood next to Mary who always sat at the table. I had a nickname for her when I wanted her to take her medication. I would call her a "goofy grape" to open her mouth. This time, Mary reached along the table to feel for me. Her hand reached my waist, and she proceeded to stand up. She then put her hands around my waist and laid her head on my chest and kissed my chest. She then took her hand and patted me on the shoulder as if to say, "Job well done," and "Thank you for going to my home and getting my medication." When Chrissy saw Mary do this, Chrissy burst into tears. Chrissy apologized for what she had said and could not believe what she had just witnessed. Prior to this, Mary never stood up without my verbal or physical prompting. I am sure that this "thank you" came from heaven.

The next day, Tuesday, my husband took care of Mary in the morning. I had to take Chrissy into Manhattan for her first sonogram at the hospital where the baby was to be born. On Wednesday, my mom and Aunt Irene took care of Mary because we had another appointment with Chrissy's new obstetrician. Aunt Irene had never met Mary before, and Mary sang several songs for her including "God Bless America." My aunt blessed her with Lourdes water as she had done hundreds of times before to my family. Aunt Irene's blessings are very special because her devotion and faith are as solid as a rock.

The rest of the week, the kids were on Easter vacation, and I would not see Mary again until the Monday after vacation. I kissed Mary goodbye as she held me in the dining room, wishing her a wonderful, restful vacation and blessed Easter.

Two days later, on Good Friday, the phone rang at 6:00 a.m. This is not unusual in our home, because my husband and I are usually up by 5:00 a.m. Since the kids were on school vacation, I had no one to get up early for that day and planned to stay in bed until Gerard got up around 6:30 a.m. I heard the phone ring but did not really pay much attention to it. Then I heard Chrissy coming up the stairs telling me that Jane was on the phone. Still half asleep, I thought that Jane needed me to babysit Mary or that something happened to Jane's mom, who was elderly and quite sick. When I got on the phone, I heard Jane crying, but it was hard to understand her. All I could hear was that Mary was dead!

I cannot describe my feelings when I heard those words. The pain in my heart was severe. I told Jane that I would be right over. When I hung up the phone, I bolted out of bed in a state that I will never be able to forget. I literally collapsed in my hallway and started to scream. Chrissy, Eddie, and my husband came running upstairs. When they heard the news, they all burst into tears and were in a state of shock. There is nothing that can prepare you for a sudden or tragic death. When it happens to a child, it is even harder to understand. At those times, you must trust in God even more. There is a reason for everything. We may not understand it at the time, but its purpose will be revealed to us eventually.

My heart was torn in two when I received that call. Now I had to pull myself together to try to bring comfort to Jane. Jane was a very private person, so this would not be an easy undertaking. When

I arrived at Jane's home, her sister and brother were with her. I had not been to their house since I got Mary's medication a few days earlier. It comforted me so much that I had gotten Mary her medication that day. In my heart, I believe that Mary may have known that Jesus was going to call her home. I will always remember the way she held me and kissed me and patted me on the back, as if she wanted to say her final goodbye to me. I never saw Mary alive after that day.

Mary had had a seizure while taking a bath and had drowned. Jane was inconsolable. Her loss as a parent was more than she could bear. Ironically, Jane and I had talked at length about our fear of dying and leaving Mary and Gerard behind. Years ago, when I was full of fear, I told Jane that I prayed to God that if I got too old to take care of Gerard, "Would he please allow us to die together?" or "Would he let me be alive when Gerard died so that I could die knowing that he had been cared for?" This was also a big fear for Jane. She lived alone and had sisters and brothers, but she had no one to entrust Mary to in the event of her death. I had mentioned to Jane that Ed and I would be willing to take Mary if that happened.

When I saw Jane in the house, we held each other and cried so hard together. Something allowed me to tell her that God had heard her prayers and her fears for Mary. God took Mary home so that Jane would not fear anymore.

Mary entered paradise in March of 2002. There is no autism or blindness in heaven. Jane's daughter now sees the radiance of heaven and sings with all the choirs of angels. She is free of any disease that might hold her back. The priest at Mary's funeral mass said the most beautiful homily for her. He said that Mary might not have met the criteria of the world, but she met the criteria of the Creator of the world. Because Mary was only sixteen and did not have the mental capacity to sin, the Catholic Church deems her eligible for sainthood. Having been baptized, Mary's soul remained pure. How lucky am I to have this sixteen-year-old saint in heaven as my friend!

I often think about the wonderful moments my family has shared with Mary. I can still hear her beautiful melodious voice singing songs in my kitchen. On nights when Jane had a meeting after work, I would take Mary off the bus and watch her until Jane picked her up. Mary loved my spaghetti and meatballs, and sometimes she could not wait for me to give her a fork. It made me laugh. Every time I make spaghetti and meatballs, I think of Mary.

The day after Mary died, I was so sad that I walked from room to room trying to find a place where I did not feel so much pain. There was no such room. Our refrigerator had a separate section just for Mary's things. It broke my heart to even look at them, so Chrissy cleaned it out for me. As upset as my children were, they kept telling me how happy they were for Mary: Mary was in paradise and beyond happy. Chrissy and Eddie kept saying that I was only crying for my own personal loss, and they were right. What helped me start to heal was that Mary did not *die*; her life had simply changed. As a devout Catholic, I believe in the resurrection, which means that, one day, if I reach heaven, I will see Mary again.

That day, I continued crying as I looked out my front window. My sisters, my mom, and Aunt Irene called me several times to see if I was all right. Even my cousin Jim called because he heard the news from Mom. Their calls meant so much to me. Katie and I had a good cry together since Katie had helped me many mornings with Mary and the family.

As I stood at the window and looked up to heaven, I asked Mary to send me a sign that she was happy and well. No sooner had I finished my prayer when the back door opened, and in walked my husband, Ed, holding something in his hand. He had been digging out a retaining wall around our pool and found a pin about two and a half feet down in the dirt. He said that it sparkled to catch his attention. At first, he thought it was a shiny rock, but when he picked it up, he realized it was a pin. When he placed it in my hand, I burst into tears. There, in my hand, was a *blue butterfly pin*! Mary used to wear white leather sneakers with *blue butterflies* embroidered on them. This sign was sent to me by Mary from heaven to confirm where she was and that all was well! This pin let me know that Mary's journey was complete, even though she was only sixteen. I hope someday, if I reach heaven, I will be able to return the embrace that Mary gave me in thanks.

Mary and Anthony would become two very strong spirits in heaven who would help my family in the next few months. After the funeral mass, I never saw Jane again. I called her at home, but she was not ready to talk to me or have a visit. When she is ready, I will always be there for her. You cannot imagine how many blue butterflies I have received since Mary's death. They are signs from Mary to remind me that she is always with me in spirit.

When William arrived that day to reconstruct the floors, I could hardly talk. William, a man who barely knew me, was soon trying to comfort me about Mary. He even told me that he would leave and return on Monday. In hindsight, I realize that the flood had a tremendous purpose. It served as a great distraction that occupied my mind during those difficult months. Having workmen come in and out of the house on a daily basis gave us the opportunity to focus on other things.

CHAPTER 26

A Miracle from Heaven

It was mid-April, and Chrissy's baby was due in May. There was still a lot of work to do and very little time left. Chrissy was very happy with her new doctors, but the trips back and forth to Manhattan took nearly two to three hours depending on the time of day and the traffic. In addition, Chrissy's medical case required quite a bit of phone coordination to set everything up. I must have made at least fifty calls to the insurance carrier and the doctors' offices. This was an expensive and serious matter that needed to be addressed. As soon as the pediatric cardiologist gave me the name of the physician for the open-heart surgery, I got on the phone with my daughter's insurance carrier. The obstetrician and the heart surgeon were both participating providers; and the hospital, which is world-famous for providing excellent care and having the most sophisticated equipment, was also approved. There are not enough words of praise and thanksgiving to God and Mother Mary for all that they have done for us. Now we needed to pray for a *special miracle* for the baby.

I planned a big baby shower for Chrissy, although some people thought we should have the shower after the baby was born in case he or she did not survive. But I call this "stinkin-thinkin." In my heart, I trusted God completely. All was well, and I would think only positive thoughts about my grandchild. How could I think anything else when I had the spirits of Anthony and Mary cheering me on in heaven—they said to *trust, and trust, and trust some more!*

In the last week of April, I threw a baby shower for Chrissy with about a hundred guests. It was lovely, and Chrissy received the most beautiful gifts for the baby. Chrissy was filled with so much joy and happiness. I had one hundred plastic rosaries blessed and attached to booklets that I had specially printed. Each booklet began with a letter to my grandchild and then followed with instructions on how to pray the Rosary. Fifty sets were pink, and fifty were blue. In the letter, I emphasized that if everyone could say just one Rosary for my grandchild's well-being, Mother Mary would bring these petitions to Jesus to be answered. Regardless of their faith, everyone left the shower with a Rosary. I purchased extra sets to hand out to anyone who could not attend the shower. Even William, the contractor, took a set to put around his truck mirror! What contractor do you know who would not only take the Rosary but display it on his vehicle? I also had masses being said around the world at various shrines for the baby. With so many people praying for the baby's safe delivery and impending surgery, it was now up to God to decide.

A week before Chrissy's pregnancy was scheduled to be induced, I received a call from the surgeon's office telling me that our insurance carrier had given me the wrong information. Here we were, in the *final* countdown, and suddenly bad news! Instead of panicking, I prayed and told God to please take care of this matter immediately. Later, the insurance carrier called and told me that they were in the midst of negotiations with the doctor's office. This was highly sophisticated surgery, and this doctor had perfected the technique. After several calls back and forth, they came to an agreement. Had I panicked, I would have wasted a lot of time and energy. Trusting in God allowed me to think clearly and remain calm.

We met the surgeon who would do the cardiac operation, and he did not sugarcoat the situation. The baby had a very serious heart defect with several troublesome components. Despite all the negative information, it was amazing on how calm and joyous Chrissy and I felt when we were in the hospital.

We visited the neonatal intensive care unit where the baby would be transferred after delivery. Here we met the most wonderful, caring, and compassionate people. One was a neonatologist who had retired but came in a few hours a week to help out. He gave us a wonderful tour of the unit and answered all our questions. When we saw the babies, it finally dawned on us that our baby would be here within two weeks—with God's help.

Another person who gave us such a sense of peace was the hospital's chaplain. He was coming off the elevator when Chrissy saw him. She told him that she wanted the baby to be baptized at birth in case the baby did not survive. When the chaplain started talking, he was filled with so much joy, especially when he was talking about the babies in the unit. He said that he came in at all hours of the night to be with the babies, particularly when they were very sick. Chrissy and I felt great goodness and peace radiating from this man.

When the chaplain took a pen out of his jacket to write down Chrissy's name and her scheduled date of delivery, Chrissy and I *gasped*; the pen was covered with *butterflies!* When he saw us looking at it in amazement, he told us that he loved butterflies because the butterfly is a sign of the resurrection. At that moment, Chrissy and I knew we were in the right place for her and the baby. We *knew* that all would be well.

After leaving the chaplain, we decided to catch a bite to eat in the cafeteria. We were given directions to walk down a corridor and cross over to another building. As we went down the corridor, we started to see hand-painted butterflies *everywhere!* They were on the walls, the ceilings, and even the floor! There was even a butterfly tree where beautiful painted butterflies were migrating to and fro. We looked at each other and had such joy in this confirmation from God. We needed to just keep the faith and pray—and that is what we did.

I went with Chrissy to have her baby on May 15, 2002. Ed and my mom stayed at home to watch the other kids. Before I left, I prayed that Mother Mary would watch over and protect them in my absence, especially Gerard. I would be away from home for two days. It was a beautiful evening when we arrived at 8:00 p.m. The room was lovely, but the view was beautiful as it overlooked the Hudson River. The sun was starting to set, making the sky radiant. Our nurses could not have been nicer or more helpful.

After I got Chrissy settled in, I took out all my small pictures of Jesus and Mother Mary, St. Anthony, St. Philomena, St. Gerard, and also my friends, Anthony and Mary. I set them up on the windowsill next to my rosaries. I was not about to leave any of them at home! We were all in this together.

The next morning, they began to induce Chrissy. She normally has a low threshold for pain, so I had expected a long scream-filled day. But Chrissy surprised me; she was quiet and calm throughout the process, even after medication to induce labor was administered. By dinnertime, she had not dilated very much, so I decided to take a walk to the cafeteria to get something to eat and make a few phone calls. Passing through the hallway with the butterflies was also a much-needed lift at this time. After gulping down my food, I made two quick calls to Ed and my mom. Everyone was praying so hard for Chrissy and the baby, and I could *feel* those prayers as I tended to Chrissy throughout the day.

When I returned to the delivery room, I noticed that the fetal monitor was flashing and sounding an alarm. Not wanting to show any apprehension to Chrissy, I glanced at the monitor. The baby's heart rate was *tachycardic* or beating at a fast rate. The food that I had just woofed down almost came right back up! Instead of going to pieces, I had promised myself that I would go through the entire event with *trust in God*. So many times I have had one foot over that finish line and then pulled back because of my lack of trust. Not this time. I could hear the voices of all my friends in heaven telling me to *finish the race*! Finish the race with that blinding trust that I had worked so hard to obtain.

I went to the windowsill and picked up my rosary. Mother Mary has never let me down, and I looked at all the pictures of my favorite friends in heaven and told them to go to the throne of God and bring my prayers to him. Chrissy's baby needed help, and if the baby's distress continued, they would do an emergency C-section. I held onto my rosary and just kept telling God that I trusted in his will and that he would do what was right.

That is just what God did. The baby's heart rate decreased to a safer level, and when Chrissy was examined, she was fully dilated and ready to push. Only the delivery nurse, the obstetrician, and I were in the room. A team of doctors waited outside the door to take the baby as soon as he or she was born. I got to hold Chrissy's leg up and coach her through the delivery. When I saw his little head coming through the birth canal, I was filled with indescribable joy. My feelings about the sanctity of life became even stronger. The pride I felt in my daughter was unbelievable. I knew that there was a rough road ahead of her, but she made the right choice; nothing of value comes from an easy path.

At 9:00 p.m. on May 16, 2002, Chrissy gave birth to a seven-pound- nine-ounce baby boy whom she named Anthony. Of course, she named him after St. Anthony since we have no Anthonys in our family. The doctor let me cut the umbilical cord and kiss him with Chrissy before they took him away. This was another amazing moment in my internal scrapbook!

One hour after he was born, I pushed Chrissy in a wheelchair to see Anthony in the neonatal unit. He already had an echocardiogram, and his color was beautifully pink as it had been when he was born. There are not enough words in the English language to thank God and Mother Mary for this blessing. All that pain we had endured as a family in the past few years was given back to us on that day with the life of baby Anthony. Of course, I had to put a picture of Mother Mary of Medjugorje on his bassinet in the unit. Her love was for *all* the children, not just for baby Anthony. I told Mother Mary to watch over every baby in the nursery.

Chrissy was discharged from the hospital two days later. She was so sad leaving the hospital without her baby. Because the metro traffic was terrible, we had to visit the hospital at odd hours. We would set the alarm clock for 2:00 a.m. and travel at 3:00 a.m. so that we could arrive at the hospital by 4:30 a.m. There was no traffic on the road at this time, so it worked out well. We would stay for a few hours each morning and then return home. Chrissy would then go right to bed to rest while I mobilized the rest of the "troops" for school. I probably averaged two to three hours of sleep daily for about a month.

On his sixth day of life, baby Anthony underwent seven hours of bypass surgery to correct his fragile and young heart. Prior to his surgery, baby Anthony had never needed to be intubated. He was doing so well that he even amazed the doctors and nurses. We called the hospital regularly to check on him, and, before each call, we said a quick Hail Mary and prayed that Anthony would continue to get well. On our travels to and from the hospital, we would say the Rosary for Anthony's recovery. Over time, the medical team gradually removed another tube or stopped another medication. They originally told us that it could be possibly *two or three weeks* before he could come home depending on his progress. But Anthony came home only *one week* after his surgery! He could have come home one day earlier, but we chose to have him circumcised.

Anthony soon became my suckilicious baby boy. I suck his little lips, nose, ears, feet, tiny butt, and the back of his little neck on a daily basis. Chrissy got a great new job after his birth, and I became the "official" babysitter. He is his Nana's angel baby. I have to remind myself that he had open-heart surgery because he is quite active. He walks in his walker so fast that I have to tell him to slow down. He has taken over the entire house and is our "little prince." My sons, who are his uncles, are crazy about him: Gerard calls him "Baby Hanthony" and kisses and holds him (with adult supervision).

This entire experience had profound effects on Chrissy. Although Chrissy was never into alcohol or drugs, we did have some trying times with her during her teenage years. Sometimes, she was so fresh and belligerent that I feared she would never mature and grow up. As a teen, Chrissy was always *running* somewhere, and our home became just a "pit stop" for her. She had too many friends, and her entire existence revolved around which friend she was going to see next. My husband and I knew her friends were all good kids, but Chrissy would not slow down. By the time Chrissy turned eighteen, I told God that he was in charge of her now. This was his child, and he needed to guide her and direct her.

It was when I surrendered "control" that Chrissy began to grow. Chrissy's pregnancy saved her. God literally stopped Chrissy in her tracks. She had to learn many lessons during her pregnancy. One of the most important was that the friends that she "could not live without" suddenly abandoned her when she became pregnant. Many times she had to have a good cry for herself. Despite the pain, it taught her a valuable lesson. Some lessons cannot be taught; they have to be lived. Chrissy could not listen to us, so God gave her a lesson through life experience so that she would really learn from him. Chrissy's pregnancy enabled her to bond with her family again. As a family, we spent the entire nine months together waiting for the baby's arrival. Although the baby's heart problems were very hard on Chrissy, the difficulties made her stronger as a woman. Once again, God shows us that what the world may consider a "problem" may actually be a "blessing."

Chrissy has become the most loving, compassionate, and responsible mother to little Anthony. When she arrives home from work, he wants to jump out of my arms to be with her. Baby Anthony has taught Chrissy how to really live. He is her greatest *gift* from God.

We were also truly blessed to have a wonderful cardiologist to care for Anthony on Long Island. Her devotion and compassion are evident every time we see her for Anthony's appointments. Anthony has no medications at this time, but his aortic artery will have to be watched carefully, requiring visits for blood pressure checks and echocardiograms. Anthony is our constant reminder that God works miracles each and every day.

CHAPTER 27

A Journey of Faith

Last July, I invited Katie and her son Patrick to go to the beach with us. We were going to the shore several times a week because the cardiologist told us that the salt air was good for healing Anthony's heart. That was all I needed to hear. So four times a week, I loaded everything we needed for the beach.

The day Katie came with us was beautiful; the sun was very hot, but there was a constant breeze. The waves were quite high, and the undertow was powerful. I am a strong swimmer, but even I had a hard time keeping my balance while standing at the edge of the surf holding Joseph's hand. Gerard was not with us because he was in a summer school program. While Eddie and Patrick went out on their boogie boards, Katie and I watched from the shore.

Katie is tall, so it takes a good-size wave to knock her off her feet. As we stood and talked, the rough surf hit her from the side and almost knocked her over. Suddenly, Katie told me that she had been experiencing numbness down her left arm and her left leg for the past two weeks. A charley horse in her left leg woke her from sleep the past several nights. When she put her earrings on that morning, she could not feel her left earlobe. She also had the feeling of a "headband" around her head but only on one side.

My first response was, "Are you kidding?" Then I told her to get out of the pounding surf. I thought she might be having ministrokes due to some type of brain abnormality. She thought I was being funny and laughed at me while she stayed in the rough waves. I asked if her husband, Fred, knew about her symptoms, and she said that he did not know, and she did not want to worry him.

Katie is of Irish heritage, so her complexion is very fair. She burns easily, and at the beach, she was getting redder and redder. Chrissy and I kept warning her to get out of the sun, but Katie said she only gets burned once a year and that she was fine. I already had a tan from going to the beach several weeks before that day, but I still got a burn over my baseline tan that day. I worried that Katie was going to have a very bad burn that night.

That evening, after I got the kids settled, I told Ed what Katie said on the beach. Ed asked me, "What will Fred do if anything ever happens to Katie and you didn't let him know beforehand?" I knew Ed was right, but I did not want to lose my friend's trust. But then I imagined her possibly stroking out at home when Fred had no idea of her symptoms. Katie might hate me now but love me tomorrow when she realizes that I told Fred only because I love her too much to let anything happen to her.

At 9:00 p.m., I called Fred and told him the whole story. Then I sat next to my phone, waiting for Katie to call back with some angry words for me. Ten minutes later, the phone rang, and it was Katie, but she was *laughing* at the other end! Apparently, she was covered in moisturizer because she could not move after getting a very *bad sunburn*! She had just covered herself in lotion and was in bed. But Fred did not care if she was covered with gold; she was going to the emergency room whether she liked it or not! Katie had a CAT scan taken at 3:00 a.m. I wonder if she loved me at that particular moment in the morning. Thankfully, her CAT scan showed no bleeding or growths, but she was now under the care of a neurologist.

Katie's symptoms disappeared three weeks later, and the neurologist ordered an MRI with a special dye. The doctor was trying to rule out multiple sclerosis. When Katie told me this, I later burst into tears. In my heart, I suddenly knew that she had MS. Her MRI showed a lesion on the brain in an area that is suggestive of MS, but at that moment, the lesion did not absorb the dye. Katie seemed optimistic, so I had to try to keep my emotions and opinions to myself.

Three months later, Katie was finally diagnosed with MS after having another MRI. This MRI did not show the lesion that had been there before, but instead there was a new lesion in a different location. When Katie came to tell me the news, we cried together and held each other. All that kept running through my mind as I hugged her was that God loved Katie so much that he wanted her to share in the blessings of carrying a cross. I told Katie that God and Mother Mary would never let her or her family down. The road may get winding and bumpy, but God would always be there to guide her path.

Katie immediately began treatment for MS. She asked if I could come to her home when the nurse came to teach her how to administer the medication. I was more than happy to be there for her. We both listened attentively to what the nurse said, and when it came time for Katie to give herself an injection in the arm, I started to cry. I was supposed to be there for my friend, to give her emotional support and comfort, but instead Katie and the nurse were comforting me! I think seeing Katie administer the injection made real for me that she had MS. For six months, Katie had no further symptoms.

In the middle of May, Katie had to have an operation for nerve compression from a herniated disc. This was not related to the MS, but it caused her to have quite a bit of pain and discomfort. She suffered from severe charley horses in both legs and could hardly walk. She needed immediate back and spinal surgery. She went through the surgery without any complications and was released the next day.

Four days after the surgery, Katie called me early in the morning. The kids had just gotten on the buses, and there was only Baby Anthony with me at home. Katie asked if I could come see her; she was not feeling well, and her husband was at work. She said that she could not seem to focus her eyes, and the room was spinning. I grabbed little Anthony, my blood pressure cuff, and a stethoscope, and ran to Katie's house.

Sitting at the kitchen table, Katie could not even focus on me! I took her blood pressure thinking that perhaps she had some bleeding from the surgery, but her blood pressure was fine as was her heart rate. When I looked at her face, her right eye was looking right over my head, and her left eye had rolled completely to the left. She kept wiping her face and eyes in an attempt to try to correct them. Knowing that her vital signs were in the normal range, I realized that this was a flare-up of her MS.

Tossing my nursing skills aside, all I wanted to do was put Katie on my lap and rock her and tell her that everything was going to be all right. I did not actually do this, so I did the next best thing: I made her something to eat. I am very good at this: you have chest pain? Why don't you lay down while I whip you up the greatest meal you've ever eaten! It is amazing what food can fix. So I made Katie a toasted roll and orange juice.

While we waited for Katie's mom and dad to take her to the hospital, I got her clothes ready. I went into her laundry room to get her some things from the dryer, but I wanted to *scream*! Here was my best friend trying so hard just to focus her eyes to see me. I felt utterly helpless. After they left for the hospital, I went home and had a good cry. Then I started to pray very hard for Katie and her family.

Katie had to be hospitalized for one week, and when they took another MRI, it showed there was a lesion on her optic nerve. Most people with this type of lesion lose their sight for a month. Katie did not lose her sight, but she had significant double vision and problems with depth perception.

When I went to see her in the hospital the next day, I had a hard time looking at her. Her face looked so different because her eyes looked so strange. Katie and I have a weird sense of humor and laugh at things that most people probably think are horrible. I teased her that she looked like the comic actor, Marty Feldman, who had big rolling eyes. Then I told her that if she thought that I was going to push her around in a wheelchair, she had better have other ideas! When you can joke and make light of a serious situation, it helps to begin the healing.

Katie later wrote me the most mushy, beautiful thank-you note. She told me that she knew the road ahead was going to be long, but that she was going to travel it with God. When I read this message, my heart sang; Katie had accepted her cross, and God and Mother Mary had wonderful gifts and lessons for her. I knew that they would turn this very difficult disease into a banquet of blessings. Katie will never be abandoned. She is blessed with a wonderfully supportive family and friends. She already knows how much I love her, and I will always be there for her no matter what. For all she has done for Gerard and me, it is my turn to lend a hand when God calls.

CHAPTER 28

Final Thoughts

Finishing this book has been harder than starting it. Writing over these past two years, I was making mental notes about what I wanted to say in this chapter. I cannot pin down the day on which I felt the need to write this book. At first, the book was only a passing thought. But through prayer, I realized that this book was a mission given to me by our Father in heaven. It is my hope that this book will encourage those who take care of someone with autism.

When Gerard was diagnosed, there was a sudden increase in the number of identified cases of autism around the country. In the following year, the number of special classes accommodating these children tripled. Today, autism has become epidemic in certain parts of the world. Although I am interested in autism's etiology, I am much more interested in how families like mine cope with this disease. Gerard came with no instruction manual, and there are no journals that give you step-by-step instructions on how to take care of an autistic child.

I know that every parent or caretaker of an autistic child has days that he or she feels will never end or days when he or she just wants to run away and never look back. But I know in my heart that this was not the way God intended us to live with autism. I wanted a different life for myself and my family, so I made a conscious decision to accept God's will and allow him to take control. I believe now that on those difficult days, God is gently knocking on your heart—so open the door and let him come in and help!

Today, it is much easier to focus on worldly concerns than to accept the challenge of following God. In my journey of faith, I have learned that God's blessings are more important than anything the world had to offer. Even though I had faith from an early age, I still needed to learn important spiritual lessons and understand my purpose in being blessed with a special child. These lessons would be repeated many times until I learned what I needed to know. I am very grateful that God has been so patient with me. If the roles were reversed, I would have given up on me a long time ago! God's steadfast support has shown me that he truly loves me and will be faithful and patient with me forever. With Gerard's autism, I have a purpose, and God will help me to fulfill it. My complete surrender of life's problems to God's will has become my saving grace. This is the most important lesson that I have learned.

When I stopped trying to control everything in Gerard's life and left it in God's hands, my own emotional wounds began to heal. Giving up control was not easy, but my life was so much harder when I thought I was traveling alone with autism. God has prepared a special journey for every single living human being. Trust in God—you are not alone on this journey.

I remember looking at the faces and listening to the stories of parents at autism support groups and hearing their fears. They were filled with anxiety and sometimes despair. Like them, I remember not feeling the inner peace and joy that fills my life now. What began my *transformation* was finding a way to talk to God more and more about my problems and struggles. This meant doing more than conventional religious practices. Of course, I had formal prayers including Sunday mass, my daily family Rosary, the Divine Mercy Novena, St. Anne's Novena, and a daily reading from the book *God's Calling*. These formal prayers were reassuring, but my most comforting prayers came in the form of *heart-to-heart talks with God*. I decided to *invite* God and Mother Mary to share every single minute of my existence.

My most productive and personal prayers occur when I visit the Blessed Sacrament in the church. I always bring two cups of tea with me, prepared in the same way: both are light with one and a half sugars. Without a doubt, God is a tea drinker who drinks tea the *same way I do*! Sometimes, in front of the tabernacle, I tease Jesus, saying that I hope he is not starting to become "cheap" because "Here I am, a guest in his house, bringing the tea, and there are no Danish or donuts to go with it!"

You may think I am a little crazy, but I assure you that I am not. This simple act of hospitality has allowed me to develop a close *friendship with God* that words cannot adequately describe. This divine friendship surpasses any human relationship because it comes from the very *source* of love without boundaries or limits. It is humans who make boundaries and build walls against love.

When I started to write this book, I had lengthy arguments with God. I thought I was making a big mistake, believing that anyone would be interested in this subject. But God revealed to me, through my own life experiences and discussions with other parents, that there was a great need for a message of hope in autism. This hope is real and available to anyone who wants inner peace and serenity.

The first step is to understand that autism is not a punishment from God. Even though living with autism can make you feel like you are being punished, it is actually the *opposite* in the Lord's eyes. I believe that the parents and caretakers of autistic children are specially handpicked in heaven. God picked the "cream of the crop" to help raise every child with a physical, emotional, or mental handicap. By specially picking you, God also promises to be with you throughout this difficult journey.

God often gets a bad reputation when terrible events happen. When things are good, we utter words of praise. Then when a difficult trial comes along, we think it is God's fault, and we reject him. But if we took the time to notice the outcome of the trial, we would be greatly surprised by its blessings. Remember, God sees the *whole picture*. His gifts are much more beautiful than we can ever anticipate or expect. God is faithful to each and every one of us, and his hand is outstretched to gently guide and direct us.

The next step is to find out what keeps you from knowing God in your life. Handle this problem the way you would correct any other physical or medical concern. We seek professional help when there is something wrong with our bodies. Likewise, if your soul is not at rest, neither are *you*! You may possess all the wealth in the world, but if you are missing your spirit, you are *not* at peace.

Most people today run around in circles looking for ways to stop their uneasiness. The insanity of the world creeps in on all of us and makes us want to escape—but running away only adds to our confusion and anxiety when we do not know God. People tend to find more comfort in following earthly solutions, but these are only short-term fixes. They are never life affirming or sustaining. Look at Hollywood with all its fame and riches and *craziness*. It is clear that the world really needs to know God better. There is nothing in this world that can ever surpass a wonderful, intimate friendship with God.

If I wanted to talk to the president or visit with a king or queen, it would not be possible unless I had a specific job or title that gave me the privilege. If I had some opportunity to meet them, it would be on *their* time and schedule. I would have to wait until they were ready to receive me. By contrast, God, the Creator of the universe, is superior to any human dignitary. His kingdom is vast and without end, and his resources are infinite. You would think someone with such power would be unapproachable. Yet God is there for each and every one of us at every moment of our lives. He is in places that no earthly king would ever dare to enter. With deepest humility, he is gladdened whenever we invite him to share in any moment of our lives.

I do not have much material wealth, but God provides for me constantly. He does not care how I look or dress. He only knows how much I truly love him and how much I need him. It is hard for us to imagine that God needs us too. He needs us to fulfill his will on earth. So when God blesses you with an autistic child, he had a definite purpose for you. He knows that this job is not easy, but he will give you rewards that more than compensate. I have come to feel *honored* that God *chose me* to be Gerard's mom and my family to be Gerard's family.

It often puzzles me when people ask how I can be so joyful with all that I have gone through. Some people have even suggested that Ed and I have a "black cloud" over us of very bad luck. This could not be farther from the truth. God did not give us these trials to punish us. He allowed them to happen so that we could all grow and learn from the experience. Every trial has turned into a blessing. We may not be able to see it at first because our human sight is so limited. When you ask God to show you his will, your limited vision is gradually replaced by a spiritual revelation that clarifies everything.

As you surrender control, God starts to remove the heavy baggage—one piece at a time. For some strange reason, we seem to like to carry extra baggage and find it more comfortable to hold onto things that weigh us down. We all become accustomed to the dysfunctional madness in our lives and think it is normal. But that craziness prevents us from knowing God. If you let God remove the baggage, he will set you free!

Many people use the same excuses to not seek God time after time. They avoid church because a priest once yelled at them in the confessional or gave them bad advice. Others think that the Church is just looking for their money. Many people say they are too busy and have everything they need. While others admit that they are not "into religion." All these excuses lead to the same outcome: separating ourselves from God, the true source of joy, love, peace, and contentment. It does not matter which religion you follow. We are all under *one God* who loves us more than words can describe.

We can see how the world is spinning out of control. Watching the news shows us that serious problems exist and the world is filled with venomous hate that cannot be quenched. People are trying to do everything faster and faster. Desire for wealth and power become the only reasons for existence. Marriages are based on how much income a spouse makes, and spouses merely tolerate each other because of financial status and security, instead of truly loving each other for their heart and character. There is *never* enough money, *never* enough power to satisfy anyone. The tragedy is that even when some people reach their "goal," they experience only apprehension, depression, and the feeling that something is missing in their lives. They think that perhaps this missing element can be purchased: a bigger home, a bigger boat, a faster car, a more grand vacation. But when the novelty wears off, they are left with a sense of confusion. This is because "stuff" cannot fill a spiritual void.

The *real* issue is our souls. Every person that comes into the world has a soul. That soul is as much a part of you as your heart and lungs. As we grow, our soul thirsts for God. The things of this world cannot quench that thirst. Only a relationship with God can satisfy this thirst. When that wish is met, your soul is fulfilled.

The final step is *trusting in God*. When I talk about trust, I am not referring to merely words. You must *live in trust of God* to have his incredible friendship. It is very hard to let go of the things that restrain you from achieving this total trust. I was only able to attain this complete trust after seeing how the world deceives us with empty promises, pain, anxiety, depression, and frustration. I decided that I did not want this empty feeling for myself or my children. Even with the difficulties of managing Gerard, my children have a home filled with love, joy, and laughter. Practicing our faith every day makes this possible. It takes a lot of hard work and dedication, but having God and Mother Mary walking by our side has allowed my family to have great blessings. I know my children will continue the tradition for their families one day. I can already see this in Chrissy who is a warm, loving, and compassionate mother. She chose to take the harder road by having her son, and she and Anthony are truly happy.

People often ask me how I learned to trust in God. I tell them that through every trial I saw God's helping hand. God did not want me to "throw in the towel." He wants me to know that he is faithful to me and will never let me down. His continual support brings tears to my eyes because it shows how deeply he loves me. He loves *each of us* in the same way. He does not care about your color or creed, your job title or educational level, your wealth or poverty—none of it matters. All that matters is that you open up your heart to his divine healing.

To all the parents, guardians, and caretakers of special children, know that you are also *special* in God's eyes. He has wonderful plans for each and every one of you. When the bad days seem long and overwhelming, know that there is true help for you. The next time your child has an outburst or episode, try asking God for help. It cannot hurt or make anything worse than it already is, and I believe you will see that things do get better.

We live in a society that has a hard time accepting suffering. We do not like pain in any form, so we run for medication at the first sight of discomfort. We also do not like to see anyone we care for suffer. But by offering these moments of suffering to the Lord, God will send you blessings. Had Gerard not been diagnosed with autism, I would never have developed the close relationships I have with my family and friends. I would certainly have never reached the level of trust and friendship I have with God, Mother Mary, and all my saint friends in heaven.

We are blessed by suffering. From suffering, we learn to be compassionate. My family and neighbors have all been blessed by Gerard's autism. An outpouring of love has come from everyone around us, and God has healed many people through Gerard. This next thought may be difficult for you to understand; if Gerard were completely healed of autism tomorrow, I might actually fear *losing my complete dependence on God!* I know, however, that my relationship with God will never change, because God will always be my faithful companion and because I will always need God's love to sustain me.

I end my book with a prayer of hope for all of you who walk this journey of autism:

> Heavenly Father, I ask you, as your daughter, to bless and strengthen all of your children on earth. Give them your strength to be able to carry the very heavy cross of autism. Free them from anxiety, depression, and despair; and fill their hearts and souls with hope, joy, and your love. Let them know of your faithfulness to us all. Teach them to remove fear from their hearts. Fill each and

every one who reads this book with your peace. It is through your peace, love, and joy that all fear is erased.

Thank you, Father, for allowing me to experience this incredible journey on earth with you. I thank you for every gift and blessing that you have sent my family and me. I also thank you for all the trials and suffering that you have allowed to come our way. They have been the key to my strength and the reason for my faith. Most of all, I thank you, Jesus, for sending me your mother to teach me the patience, love, and understanding needed to care for Gerard. Thank you, Mary, for all your gentle molding and guidance. This has allowed me to see and love others in a different light. Thanks to all my great saint friends in heaven, along with those who have already gone home. One day, my name will be called, and I will be among you in paradise.

Father, I thank you for all those people who have made my cross lighter with their support and love. I especially thank you for my mom and dad, Aunt Irene, and my Nan, who all taught me my faith. I thank you for my faithful and loving sisters and brothers-in-law. Thank you so much for my nieces and nephews. Thank you for my family that walks the walk with me each and every day: my husband Ed and my kids, Chrissy, Eddie, Gerard, and Joseph. Hugs and kisses for the blessing of our grandbaby Anthony. Thank you for my cousin Ann, who has been a constant source of support for both Gerard and me. Thank you, Lord, for sending us such wonderful friends and neighbors who have helped us throughout these difficult years. Jesus, I especially thank you for sending me Dr. Z——. If it had not been for him, this book would not have been possible. Thank you also for sending me little Mary to watch over and to take care of. May "Mayor Anthony" and "Little Mary" reap rewards in heaven greater than they ever hoped. I offer this prayer to you in the name of Jesus, through the intercession of Mary, for the glorification of God the Father in heaven.

Love and a billion hugs and kisses,
your daughter Elizabeth XXXOOO.

To my readers, you and I may never actually meet in this lifetime, but we are connected spiritually through the blessing of autism. One day, we will all meet in paradise. May God and Mother Mary bless you on your journey! Give God a chance to help you; it will be the greatest trip you will ever take. Leave the baggage at the curb, and let yourself start to really live. Keep on track, stay the course, and keep the faith alive!

ABOUT THE AUTHOR

 Elizabeth Nabet remains active in spending quality time with her four children and their families. This includes her five grandchildren. Her two youngest children, Gerard and Joseph, are both diagnosed in the autism spectrum. Joseph is high functioning with Asperger's syndrome.

Gerard entered a group home in December 2014, one month after the sudden passing of Elizabeth's husband, Ed, in November 2014.

Her time is divided between caring for her family and teaching at her Church's Faith Formation in preparing second graders for receiving their first Holy Communion. She has a true passion for cooking and baking for family, friends, and the group home where Gerard resides.